THE GLASS ENCLOSURE

The Life of Bud Powell

by

Alan Groves

and Alyn Shipton

Recording Chronology by Alyn Shipton

CONTINUUM

New York • London

2001

The Continuum International Publishing Group Ltd
The Tower Building, 11 York Road, London SE1 7NX

The Continuum International Publishing Group Inc
370 Lexington Avenue, New York, NY 10017-6503

Originally published in 1993 by Bayou Press Ltd. Reprinted in 1993, 1995.
Reprinted in 2001 by Continuum by arrangement with Bayou Press Ltd.

British Library Cataloguing-in-Publication Data

A catalogue record for this book is available from the British Library.

ISBN 0-8264-4746-5 (paperback)

Library of Congress Cataloging-in-Publication Data

Groves, Alan.
    The glass enclosure : the life of Bud Powell / by Alan Groves and Alyn Shipton; recording chronology by Alyn Shipton.
        p. cm.
    Reprint. Originally published: Oxford : Bayou Press, 1993.
    Includes bibliographical references, discography, and index.
    ISBN 0-8264-4746-5 (pbk.)
    1. Powell, Bud.   2. Jazz musicians—United States—Biography.   I. Title: Life of Bud Powell. II. Shipton, Alyn.   III. Title.
    ML417.P73 G76 2001
    786.2'165'092--dc21

                                                                                    2001028002

Designed by DMC Design Associates, London
Typeset by Vitaset, Paddock Wood, Kent and CompuDesign

CONTENTS

ACKNOWLEDGEMENTS

The authors would like to thank Barry Kernfeld and the staff of the *New Grove Dictionary of Jazz* and the Music Library of Pennsylvania State University, State College, PA, for help in tracking down material from *Jazz Magazine*. Howard Rye has also helped with material from several periodicals. Thanks are also due to David Horn, Paul Oliver, and the University Library of Exeter for material from *Le Jazz Hot* and *Jazz Monthly* and other publications held in the Popular Music Archive. Barry McRea has helped by making available rare early recordings by Powell. Anne Macdonald helped in the preparation of the final text, based on a full draft by Alan Groves, edited and supplemented with material by Alyn Shipton.

PREFACE

'I wish [be-bop] had been given a name more in keeping with the seriousness of purpose.'

Bud Powell

Bud Powell and Thelonious Monk were the two most significant pianists of the style of modern jazz that came to be known as bop. Both men changed the conception of jazz piano. They started out in the same direction, with the younger Powell something of a disciple of Monk, and then diverged, as Monk explored his patterns and variations in composition, while Powell developed a solo voice supreme in live performance.

The special relationship between Powell and Monk lasted throughout Powell's life. In April 1961, I went to hear Bud while he was appearing at the Blue Note in Paris. He was overweight, sullen and unapproachable, given to staring silently at the wall, twiddling his fingers when not playing. He sat virtually motionless, and it was only his hands that moved when he did play. He appeared to have no interest in his surroundings, and little interest in his music.

Suddenly he came alive, alert and animated. Monk had come into the club with the rest of his quartet. The group was to appear at the Paris Olympia the next night, Tuesday, the day I was to return to England.

The aloof and detached Monk, complete with dark glasses and hat, was suddenly as excited as Powell. Bud finished his set, and went over to sit with the four. He and Monk chatted and giggled like children while Monk's sidemen smiled indulgently. The Blue Note's visiting guest that week was J. J. Johnson, the trombonist, but he was pointedly ignored. Similarly, the drummer Kenny Clarke (like Powell, also resident in France at that time) was a regular player at the Blue Note and was in the group accompanying Johnson. Powell had not seemed to notice him during the week of my visit and Monk now appeared not to want to notice him either.

Later, Monk sat at the piano and played solo, to Powell's apparently awestruck pleasure. After that, Powell was reluctant to continue playing. He obviously needed such a contact with a musician he trusted and admired. It was almost an embarrassment that for a few moments the inner souls of these two hidden but innovative men were revealed in public. Both pianists had immersed themselves so totally in their music that they had little life or interest outside it; both had retained total affinity, touching the depths of being in each other that no one else was allowed to approach.

ALAN GROVES

CHAPTER 1

UPBRINGING AND COOTIE WILLIAMS

Earl 'Bud' Powell was one of the supreme masters of jazz piano. Although his short life spanned only forty-two years, he was also one of the most creative and influential musicians to grace the art of jazz. Born in 1924, he was to come of age musically and physically in the early 1940s and develop into one of the founders and leading figures of the revolutionary style of modern jazz known as bop.

Between 1946 and 1953 he outshone virtually all his contemporary modern jazz musicians in technique, emotional drive and invention. His unique brilliance as a keyboard artist meant that his essence as a player was hard to recapture or copy, and, while he influenced many other musicians, few were able to emulate his style accurately. His name was made quickly in jazz circles, though hardly beyond them, and he was able to work and record regularly throughout his life; frequently, however, he was prevented from doing so by serious ill-health.

Most of the other principal founders of the modern jazz revolution of the 1940s have come to be acknowledged with wide, if belated, respect. Such musicians include Charlie Parker, Dizzy Gillespie, Fats Navarro, Thelonious Monk and Kenny Clarke. But Powell remains on the periphery. He is a shadowy presence, usually mentioned only in passing. For all his standing in the eyes of those attuned to his particular talents, his erratic personality and troubled life caused him to be something of an embarrassment; his ability and achievements have all too often been glossed over or overlooked.

From 1945, Powell suffered frequent nervous and physical collapses which interrupted his life and career for months at a time. In effect, these difficulties with his health were to rob him of about one-third of his adult life. After the first brief flowering of his talent as a pianist, much of the subsequent attention paid to him in the jazz and popular press concerned the protracted decline of the man and his music; a twenty-year struggle against the world, fought in public.

In many respects Powell's supreme achievement and contribution to his art had been made by the early 1950s. This had, nevertheless, created enough interest in his work to allow him to keep a career of sorts going thereafter; even so, his ability to continue to work during his later years was, at least in part, a consequence of the attention (and sometimes notoriety) his name commanded. His well-documented public scenes and his stays in various hospitals are perhaps the best-recorded parts of his life. The causes of his mental troubles remain obscure, as do many of the details concerning his early life and his family circumstances as he grew older.

He was born Earl Powell to a musical family in New York City on 27 September 1924. His grandfather learned guitar in Cuba. His father, William, was a respected stride pianist and bandleader. His older brother, William Jr. (Bill), played violin and trumpet, while his other brother, Richard (or Richie), also played piano.

His father was to remember:

> I tell you when Bud was seven, the musicians would come and actually steal him, take him from place to place playing music. Nobody had ever seen a jazz musician that young, or heard one play like Bud. He was a li'l' old chubby fellow, and by the time he was ten he could play everything he'd heard by Fats Waller and Art Tatum.
>
> Music just came natural in this family. My daddy was a guitar player. He went to Cuba during the Spanish-American war, and when he came back, he was one of the greatest flamenco guitarists in the country. I played piano. I taught Bud on that old upright play-o-tone there. I couldn't go on the road and have a family too. So I stayed home. But Bud was a genius. When he was just a little fellow, they'd come and steal him, and make him play sometimes to two or three o'clock in the morning. When he was just a little fellow . . .

Bud Powell started studying the piano at the age of six. Until his mid-teens, he concentrated on European classical music, especially the works of Mozart. He was to say: 'During those years I had much advice, inspiration and encouragement from my father who was a fine pianist.' The pianist Elmo Hope was a close childhood friend; they practised and listened to classical records together. Curiously, late recordings of Hope's work were to sound like a rough draft of Powell's. Hope, a less able musician, led the typical obscure, scuffling, shortened life of the modern jazz musician of the 1940s.

Powell became interested in jazz only in his early teens. His first influence was Billy Kyle, who was then the pianist with John

An early photograph of the young Bud Powell.

Kirby's small band (curiously, Powell was to work with this group himself for a short time in 1945). For three years, like many other significant jazz musicians, Powell attended De Witt Clinton High School in the Bronx, leaving at fifteen to concentrate on music. His older brother Bill became the trumpet-leader of a band in 1938–9, and Bud played piano for him. The band played for a time in the Coney Island area. Working in a jazz or dance band helped to motivate Bud to leave school to concentrate on a career in music.

We know that by 1940 he was playing solo piano in clubs such as The Place (later the Limelight Coffee Shop) in Greenwich Village, and that he played for the actor Canada Lee at the Chicken Coop in Harlem. He also worked for the female trumpeter and singer Valaida Snow in the early 1940s. She ran a band called the Sunset Royal Entertainers, and this must have flourished after she was deported from Sweden in 1941 and returned to the United States. Indeed, as a consequence of her deportation, her career didn't really begin again until her April 1943 debut at the Apollo Theatre in New York, and it is probable that Powell played with her at about this time. He must have left her well before she moved to California in 1945.

After his evenings working as a solo pianist, in common with many other New York musicians, Powell would go uptown (to Harlem) to tour the bars and nightclubs. It was in one of these that he met Thelonious Monk, who was to take him to Minton's Playhouse and involve him in the style of modern jazz which was being developed there. Powell was to be only an occasional sitter-in at Minton's during the height of the experimentation to create this new music between late 1940 and the early part of 1942.

During the years 1943–4, Powell spent a period in Cootie Williams's big band. As Bud was still under twenty-one, Williams became his legal guardian during the time he was with the band.

Charles 'Cootie' Williams had formed his big band in late 1941, after eleven years as a member of the Duke Ellington Orchestra and almost a year spent with Benny Goodman. Williams's band lasted for most of the 1940s (although it became a small group in 1948) and for much of that time it was resident at New York's Savoy Ballroom. The band came into existence almost simultaneously with the ban on recordings operated by the American Federation of Musicians, which meant that its earliest session in March 1942 was not followed by another period of recording until early in January 1944. By the time of the sessions made by a six-piece group drawn from the orchestra on 4 January, Bud Powell was a member of the band. The personnel for these first recordings is that of an all-star group. In addition to Williams on trumpet (and vocals) and Powell on piano, the members were the tenor saxophonist Eddie 'Lockjaw' Davis, the bassist Norman Keenan, both of whom were later to spend many years with the Count Basie Orchestra, and Eddie 'Cleanhead' Vinson on alto saxophone and vocals. The repertory consisted very largely of blues-styled work, and, much like the contemporaneous Earl Hines Orchestra, the organisation was a melting pot for survivors of the earlier era of jazz and swing and the younger generation of musicians amongst whom could be counted Powell himself.

Trumpeter Valaida Snow, with whom Powell played around 1943.

Two days later, the sextet returned to the studio, and at this session on 6 January the full big band also recorded. Its ranks included such old-time swing musicians as the trombonist George Stephenson and the alto saxophonist Charlie Holmes. Some of the band's arrangements were swing classics, such as Don Redman's version of *Things Ain't What They Used To Be* (Hit 7084). Others had a rhythm-and-blues flavour, such as Eddie Vinson's rendition

Cootie Williams, leading his big band in which Powell played piano 1943–4.

of the Louis Jordan hit *Is You Is Or Is You Ain't My Baby?* (Hit 7108), although Vinson takes the tune desperately slowly and almost loses momentum, not sufficiently compensated for by the fire of his alto playing.

Bud Powell is relatively overshadowed in both the small group and the big band, but he takes solos on several tunes, notably the big-band versions of *Somebody's Gotta Go* (Hit 7119) and *Blue Garden Blues* (a remake of the dixieland standard *Royal Garden Blues*; Hit 7108), both recorded some months later in August 1944. In these, his linear right-hand solo style is fully established, and it is quite clear that he had already thought out much of his approach to jazz piano playing.

His most important influence on Williams was to persuade him to record the Thelonious Monk composition *'Round Midnight* (Hit 7119, 22 August 1944). Even if Cootie Williams claimed co-composer credits with Monk for the privilege of recording the tune, it is generally reckoned to be the influence of Powell that led to its being recorded by so important a swing musician in the first place. Powell later told Francis Paudras that sections of the tune as recorded by Williams had, in fact, been composed by Dizzy Gillespie.

In May 1944, Williams's band went to Hollywood, made further recordings, and appeared in a film 'short'. During this period, Charlie Parker joined the saxophone section as well as recording a sextet *The Boppers* (Connoisseur Rarities, CR522). Powell is clearly visible in the film (made for Official Films), which has good solos from Williams, Vinson and Sam 'The Man' Taylor on *Theme* and *Wild Fire*. Williams recalled this period in an interview with Stanley Dance, particularly referring to the time both Parker and Powell were in the band: 'One night, maybe, they'd give me a lot of trouble. Maybe the next night too. But the one after, they play so fine and so great it would all even out . . .'

At the beginning of his stay with Williams, the augury for Powell's future career could hardly have been more promising: not yet twenty-one, he had the piano chair in one of the leading big bands of the mid-1940s; his family musical tradition and early talent had ensured a sound grounding as a pianist and a musician; and he was working with some of the finest names in swing and jazz. His out-of-hours associations with other musicians preoccupied with the development of modern jazz gave him a common ground with those who were searching for a new voice in black popular music, and Powell had all the talent and musical knowledge to become part of that search for a voice.

By the spring of 1945 he had left Williams's band, precipitated by an event of such magnitude that it altered his whole life. (This

The Savoy Ballroom, New York, where Cootie Williams's band was frequently resident.

will be dealt with in the next chapter.) The rest of his career was spent playing in nightclubs in small groups. His unstable mental condition meant that, from the mid-40s onwards until he settled in Paris in 1959, he rarely left the New York area to work. Until about 1950, he worked or recorded with other leaders (these included Miles Davis, Dizzy Gillespie, Charlie Parker, John Kirby, Don Byas, J. J. Johnson, Dexter Gordon, Allen Eager, Sonny Stitt and Sid Catlett amongst others). Working for others, he could be difficult, defying the bandleader's choice and conception of music. After 1950 he usually worked only with his own trio; rarely was he part of other groups, and these were generally specially organised all-star ensembles, such as the Quintet of the Year in 1953. Apart from a visit to Europe with the 'Birdland' concert package in 1956 and an appearance at the Essen Jazz Festival in 1960, Powell was largely absent from the international touring circuit (which became staple employment to many of his contemporaries). He was to return from Paris to New York in August 1964 to play at Birdland, and his last important performance was at a Town Hall concert the following spring. He died in 1966. The cause of his death was reported as a combination of alcoholism, tuberculosis and malnutrition; the press at the time did not mention anything to do with drug addiction.

Before going on to look at the events which led to Bud's

departure from the Cootie Williams Band, and many of his subsequent mental and physical troubles, we can learn something of his early years by considering the period in which he grew up.

He was born slightly before the Great Depression. Of all the economic factors that altered the life of New York black people, the depression which began with the Wall Street crash in the late 1920s was one of the biggest, and a turning point in their community. Established early in the century, the largely black areas of Harlem in the north of Manhatten suffered a rapid and total decline from the late 1920s. Harlem became a poor, overcrowded section and poverty inevitably led to rundown buildings and disease. Without money, the population had no mobility. Although the intellectual renaissance which had brought black writers and artists to Harlem during the 1920s continued in some measure, the most significant movement of the early 1930s was the growth of religious organisations. In the early years of the 1930s there were 160 churches in Harlem alone, many of them occupying storefront sites, often jostling one another cheek by jowl. The musical traditions of Harlem were also emergent during this period. At the largest level there were the theatres and dance halls; there were also the small clubs and speakeasies which had developed during the era of prohibition; and at the most domestic level of all there was the rent party, the phenomenon by which people short of the rent organised a party where people bought tickets for the privilege of soul food and the opportunity to hear a solo pianist of distinction. Many pianists worked the Harlem rent-party circuit for a living, and the most famous were Luckey Roberts, James P. Johnson, Fats Waller and Willie 'The Lion' Smith. The style of solo piano playing which developed from this was known as stride piano, and was a unique Harlem derivative of ragtime.

For Bud Powell, a black musician growing up in New York, and particularly as the son of a stride pianist, the styles of Harlem stride and swing piano were part of his upbringing. During the years of his adolescence, swing small groups and big bands came to prominence. Jazz pianists developed their work from the dixieland or traditional ensembles of the late 1920s, and the black pianists associated with the big bands developed styles which could be seen as a musical platform for the later evolution of be-bop.

For black people, music was one of the few routes out of the economic and social difficulties created by the Depression. There were active theatre and music hall circuits, on which black musicians found ready work. Similarly the big bands and territory bands (which worked mainly in the South-west) toured the United States playing for dances and one-night social engagements.

The young Bud Powell, around the time of his stint with Cootie Williams.

Although there was a dramatic decline in the activity of the American recording industry in the years between 1929 and 1932 or 1933, the emergence of radio, and particularly the number of local radio stations that were prepared to present live music, continued to give work opportunities to many musicians, white and black.

During the 1930s the black big bands such as those of Cab Calloway, Earl Hines, Duke Ellington, Count Basie and Jimmie Lunceford all saw considerable success. Perhaps they did not achieve the enormous popularity of the white bands of Benny Goodman and Artie Shaw, but they were hugely popular with the black public and had broken through to reach a wider audience. Nevertheless it was the very years in which Bud Powell began working as a professional musician that began to see the end of the big-band era. To some extent it was World War II which finally ended the remarkable dominance of the big swing bands. Musicians were drafted into the forces and other sources of employment were created which further damaged the bands.

18

When the war was over, there was a recession as the economy cooled down, yet at the same time musicians were no longer satisfied with pre-war wages. With musicians demanding a living wage at a time when it was more and more difficult to hire orchestras of considerable size, the big bands were effectively priced out of existence. In addition, the two recording bans which were brought into force by the AFM, the first from 1942 to 1944 and the second in 1948 (beginning on 1 January and finishing early in 1949), sealed the fate of these large bands. Powell's career in Cootie Williams orchestra began with the first recording ban, and extended into the years between the two periods of AFM protest. Nevertheless, although Powell's musical emergence coincided with the final years of the big bands, in the lull between the two recording bans, it also coincided with the most fertile period of the New York jam session. This was a phenomenon that dated from the development of musicians' meeting places in the early years of the century.

Historically musicians had always had their own informal meeting clubs, and in New York the first for black players was the Clef Club. This had been organised in 1910 by James Reese Europe, at the time of a large migration northwards by black people from the southern states of the USA. The Clef Club was on West 53rd Street, and served as a meeting place, booking office and rehearsal room. Many leaders assembled bands from musicians who used the Clef Club as an informal employment agency. When Harlem became a black section of New York, the Rhythm Club, which was on 132nd Street and Seventh Avenue, served a similar function in the social and economic life of musicians. These clubs, or the drinking establishments and speakeasies near them, played host to numbers of jam sessions. The New Orleans guitarist Danny Barker (who came to New York in 1930) recalls many a jam session at the Rhythm Club, often involving some of the most significant jazz musicians in New York. For pianists the rent-party tradition and the atmosphere of the jam session encouraged the development of prodigious technique. The Harlem stride piano players combined classical finesse with a formidable array of jazz styles.

By the early 1940s, the finest player at after-hours jam sessions in New York was Art Tatum. His extraordinary technical command, his remarkable ear and his mental flexibility put him in a class by himself. He was nearly blind, but this did not affect his remarkable keyboard technique, and he could hold his own anywhere in a cutting contest. Having arrived in New York in 1932, aged twenty-two, by the mid-1930s he had become unrivalled. Exhibiting the final sophistications of stride, he believed his

Art Tatum (centre) with his trio: Slam Stewart (bass) and Everett Barksdale (guitar).

strongest influence to have been Fats Waller. His style was made up of arpeggios, discursive harmonic play, and interludes that came out of time between fast, swinging stride passages. He spent many of the last thirteen years of his career playing in a trio with either guitar and bass or bass and drums. His extension of the swing technique as a soloist found its ultimate expression in the work of Oscar Peterson, perhaps his foremost disciple. Bud Powell, too, admired the dexterity of Tatum and was sometimes to echo his style when playing ballads.

If the skill of Art Tatum was one of the major influences on Powell, in the sense of endless, effortless flowing lines of improvisation, there were other pianistic influences on him too. From their work in big bands, on recordings and on broadcasts, the playing of Earl Hines and Billy Kyle became familiar to Powell, and had an equally important effect. Earl 'Fatha' Hines had come to prominence in Chicago in the 1920s during his association with Louis Armstrong. His accomplished piano solo style was daring in the improvisatory forms it employed, and embodied the 'trumpet style', in which Hines cunningly used octaves in the right-hand parts to emphasise melodic lines, giving a shouting effect similar to

Billy Kyle (left: seen here with Baron Timme Rozencrantz and Helen Oakley) was a major influence on Powell's piano style.

the trumpet or other brass. Alternative derivations of this term have been given, some more or less descriptive of the effect, but, whatever the most accurate definition of 'trumpet style', Hines was a major and significant influence on both solo jazz piano and the role of the piano in jazz ensembles.

As the swing era progressed, other changes, principally those brought about by Count Basie and Teddy Wilson, both of whom lightened the left-hand part and played sparse right-hand figures, led to a very different approach to the keyboard. The pianist Allen Tinney recalled: 'I liked Billy Kyle also – the style of Fatha Hines, with the one finger hitting at the bass theme, and then hitting something else.'

Tinney used to accompany Bud Powell on the nightclub circuit. He, Powell, and another pianist, Gerald Wiggins, used to go from club to club, hoping to sit in and compete with one another at the keyboard. Tinney recollected: 'We used to walk into different clubs, just the three of us, like three hoods. The minute a piano player would spot us he'd think "God, there goes my job." But we weren't really after a job, we just wanted to get the guy. And one of us would get whoever it was. We'd all sit down and play.'

At this period in the mid-1940s, while Powell was touring Harlem nightspots, he had already developed a reputation for being argumentative and pugnacious. Tinney recalled that Bud was 'obnoxious at times, but with me he was alright.' Tinney also remembered that Powell's mother had asked him to keep an eye on Bud because he showed signs of incipient alcoholism. Like other pianists, though, Tinney admired Powell because he was already so involved in his music that little else mattered in his life.

The pianist (and later jazz educator) Billy Taylor recollected that when he first met Powell on arriving in New York in 1944 he would get caught up in real 'knock-down, drag-out' arguments.

Within a couple of years (although after Powell's departure from the Cootie Williams Band) the pianist Mary Lou Williams was also charged with looking after Powell. (Like Cootie Williams, who remembered Bud as being sixteen when he joined the band, Mary Lou has him a couple of years younger than he would actually

Thelonious Monk (foreground) at the piano in a famous 1944 photograph of Coleman Hawkins's band on 52nd Street. Left to right: Hawkins, Benny Harris, Don Byas, Denzil Best and Eddie Robinson.

have been at this time.) She reminisced: 'I met Bud Powell when he was eighteen, a little bit after he'd left Cootie Williams's band. We became friends right away. I thought his playing was terrific. Fantastic. He used to come to the house and play, play, play. And I was the only one who could do things for Bud. Bud had a tendency to go overboard; I'd make him take a bath or go to sleep.'

Slightly later in his career, the Birdland club offered Mary Lou Williams $75 a week to take care of Powell. She turned them down on the grounds that she couldn't survive on that kind of money to sit in the house, but she offered her help when it was needed. For a time Mary Lou, together with Thelonious Monk and Powell, formed another inseparable trio. 'When Bud came to me for help, and if he got a little bit out of line, I'd say: "I'll tell Monk." He'd say: "Don't do that, baby doll." He respected Monk, he was crazy about Monk. We were going to do three-piano things. The three of us rehearsed on one piano and that was so funny. Yes it was a very happy time.'

Happy time or not, Powell used much of the period during which he worked with the Williams band to become increasingly involved with the circle of musicians who were trying to extend the boundaries of jazz. Just as there were hints of revolution in Powell's own life – from the desperate challenging of other musicians in nightclubs, to the hints of pugnaciousness and alcoholism, to the need for Mary Lou Williams to take care of him – so there were also stirrings towards revolution in the lives of many swing-era musicians, and in the late 1930s many of them were developing along similar lines. Hints of the harmonic excitement and complexity of modern jazz are present in the work of the saxophonist Lester Young, the trumpeter Roy Eldridge, the bassist Jimmy Blanton and the guitarist Charlie Christian. Milt Hinton, the bass player with Cab Calloway, recalls how he and Dizzy Gillespie would start to develop unusual harmonies in after-hours practices on the rooftops of theatres. The work of all these men can be seen as pointing to a new music, and hints of the new harmonies can be heard on many records from the late 1930s. The new style was less a revolution than a logical progression. Bop evolved from the big bands: it was sought on the working bandstand and developed in the after-hours session. It was stirring all over the United States but its evolution was soon concentrated in the clubs of New York. The founders of this new music soon found one another, and they gathered to play together to try and realise the music they could hear in their minds. The focal point of their activities rapidly became a converted run-down restaurant in the Hotel Cecil building on Harlem's 118th Street. It was called Minton's Playhouse.

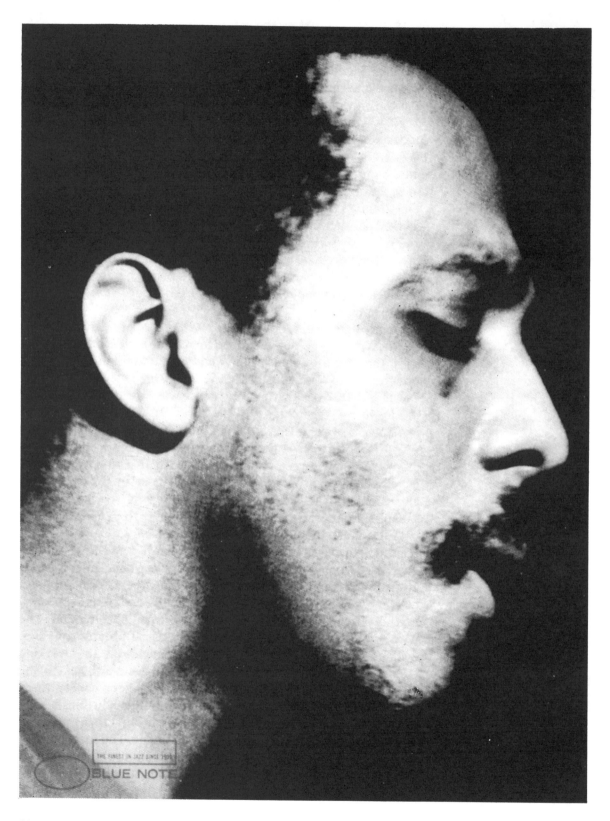

CHAPTER 2

MINTON'S AND THE FIRST BREAKDOWN

In 1940 Henry Minton was aged about fifty. He was a former saxophonist who had once owned the Rhythm Club, and had been the first black delegate to Local 802, the New York chapter of the American Federation of Musicians. Minton ran the Playhouse by himself until late 1940. Until that point it was a quiet gathering place for his friends from the dance and big-band business. He was generous with loans and 'loved to put a pot on the range' to feed his unemployed friends. He also encouraged jam sessions. At one time there was a small band in the back room led by the tenor saxophonist Happy Caldwell, although apparently there was often no music to be heard, and the house piano would frequently go untouched for several days.

In the late 1930s and early 1940s most of the trade for the Playhouse came from the Hotel Cecil itself. There was a connecting door from the club to the hotel's lobby and in more prosperous times the clubroom had been the hotel dining room. Business declined for the club in the early 1940s, and Minton hired a manager to improve its circumstances. He chose the ex-bandleader Teddy Hill. A saxophonist who had performed on all the reed instruments, Hill had also played drums and trumpet. He had a background in variety, having toured with the Whitman Sisters' show, and had later worked in several New York clubs. His taste for management had been developed when he played for Luis Russell's orchestra (between 1928 and 1929) and helped to run the band. Later, after working with James P. Johnson, he led his own big band from 1932. He was a regular feature in Harlem, and appeared often at the Lafayette Theater, the Savoy Ballroom and the Ubangi Club. After a tour of Europe in 1937 he returned to the United States, and led his own band until shortly before he joined forces with Henry Minton to run the nightclub.

It was Hill's idea to promote the jam session as a regular part of

Francis Wolff's famous photograph of the young Bud Powell taken just after the period described in Chapter 2 at the time of Bud's 1949 recordings for Blue Note.

the club's attraction. It was also his idea to put on a Monday night buffet for the artists in the stage show at the Apollo Theatre. Monday night was their night off, and he put a notice on their callboard inviting everyone in the cast. Mondays at Minton's quickly went beyond being an evening for local names and became a celebrity night. At the same time, Hill went out of his way in the buffet dinners to offer soul food: red beans and rice, sweet potato pie, collard greens, panfried chicken, barbecued ribs and creole sauce and candied yams. From time to time he went to the expense of flying in the delicacy of crawdads from Kansas City, or Mississippi catfish from St Louis.

Hill saw that attitudes were changing in jazz, that new ideas were being pushed by the young generation. He understood, at last, that the young musicians came from a different world of experience from that of the older men. Unlike their elders, many of these newcomers had been formally trained in music and were looking for new experiences. Hill wanted to attract these musicians to the Playhouse, although he did not want to lose the established names. Additionally he wanted to do something for the men who had worked for him, seeing himself as something of a benefactor for them in hard times. For the house-band, he hired a rhythm section to be fronted by one solo instrument. This would be the basic unit, acting as an invitation to those who wanted to join in and jam. He engaged the drummer Kenny Clarke to play with the band, the same man whom he had fired a year before from his own band for being 'too modern'.

Whilst Clarke had been playing with the Hill band, his new concepts in drumming had unsettled his fellow musicians. He had taken the pulse of the beat from the bass drum to the top cymbal, leaving him free to use the bass and snare drums for explosive accents, known as 'dropping bombs' or 'kicks'. His shifting, jagged patterns over his regular beat were justified as necessary spurs to soloists, who, given to creating longer lines, needed more help from the drummer. His nickname was 'Klook-a-mop', later shortened to 'Klook': this was an affectionate onomatopaeic representation of his favourite percussive figure. According to jazz legend, Hill had fired Clarke after telling him to keep the beat on the bass drum where it belonged; he also told Clarke that people did not want to hear that kind of thing, and that they wanted music they could dance to. Now, at Minton's, the prime concern for the bandleader-turned-manager was attracting the younger musicians. He was never again to try and influence the musicians about what they should play; the character of the music was to change as the new men gathered and encouraged each other to experiment. At first, Clarke expressed surprise when asked by Hill to be the house drummer. Then, realising that Hill wanted to encourage musicians who were thinking along similar lines to himself, Clarke suggested that Hill hire as house pianist the strangely named Thelonious Sphere Monk.

Monk was a tall, heavy young man, withdrawn and puzzled by life away from the piano. He tended to appear in public wearing dark glasses or one of a remarkable collection of hats. He was self-taught and lived at home with his doting, widowed mother. He had a mirror attached to the ceiling above the household's piano so he could study the action of the keyboard, the strings and the hammers. Monk spent hours practising at home, at any hour of the day or night, and explored the sounds that the piano could make. His style was based on chords which included unexpected intervals. Sometimes he would produce strings of twelve notes struck simultaneously, using all his fingers and with each thumb hitting two keys together; he even used his elbows to add extra notes of dissonance, and his jagged swing meshed with Clarke's. Both men produced new sounds that were different from one another and from what had gone before, but both worked together. Monk had already written the modern classics *Blue Monk*, *'Round Midnight* and (with Clarke) *Epistrophy*.

The guitarist Danny Barker recalled: 'The purpose in the beginning at Minton's was to manipulate the sounds and chord and harmonic structures of the songs played there. At Minton's, and in a few other backrooms, strategy was planned and plotted, gradually taking form, to cut out and eliminate inferior players. Thelonious Monk was the leader of the Minton's bandstand (a very small, tight one). He generally started playing strange introductions going off, I thought, to outer space . . .'

Barker remembered how, after Monk's extended introductions, a rim shot on the drum from Kenny Clarke would set the band going in 'a mind-boggling diffusion of rhythms and sounds.'

For such a lively club, and such a developmental centre for the new music, the atmosphere was unusual. Barker said: 'In Minton's there was complete quiet: very little talking, no glasses clinking, no kinds of noises. Everybody intent in observing and figuring out the music and the behaviour of the players, especially of the musicians who dared to jump into the arena.'

Hill was exasperated by the eccentric Thelonious Monk. To some extent, Monk appeared to behave in a singular manner to keep people at their distance. He was said to fall asleep at the house piano when practising out of club hours, then waken with a start and immediately begin to play. He would stand on street corners, immobile for hours, literally watching the world go by. Whilst Hill found him irresponsible and undependable, he had seldom met anyone so likeable. Hill complained that even if Monk had arrived early for the first set of the night, due to begin at 10.00 pm, he might then go missing and be found perhaps writing music in the club's kitchen long after the set had begun. Monk would get so absorbed in writing that he would not hear anything of the music from next door.

Accounts vary as to the exact membership of the band. To start with, it appears to have been completed by Nick Fenton on bass and Joe Guy on trumpet. Later the personnel changed, the bass was abandoned and a second front-line instrument, usually an alto saxophone, was added.

Minton's, physically and structurally, was a dull, drab place. In the fashion of the time a marquee extended from the kerb to the entrance. The kerb was painted white and zoned as a passenger loading area. Inside the club was a checkroom, a long bar, tables, a wall with old, worn mirrors, and a cramped bandstand. Beside the bandstand the wall was covered with murals, some of which showed people playing, sitting on a bar or talking; behind the band was an abstract mural of waves and clouds. The stand itself had a small Lester grand piano and a drumset, with about enough standing room for five or six musicians. Above the stage were hung curtains in folds. The club was poorly lit, cheap, and clean enough. Minton frequently redecorated the premises.

To start with the jam sessions attracted the principal musicians of the swing era. In much the same way as at the Rhythm Club, name bandleaders themselves turned up to play, to sit in, or just to listen. These included Ellington, Andy Kirk, Count Basie, Lionel Hampton, Earl Hines, and the white bandleaders Artie Shaw and Benny Goodman.

The members of the young rhythm section were not as rigid in their methods as might be expected – at least to start with. Clarke recalled that they were pleased to have Goodman, who was still then all the rage, in the club. He remembered that they changed their style to accommodate his, so that Goodman could play what he wanted, not what might be forced on him. Sometimes there was a guest rhythm section to conform to the style of a particular visitor. Transitional figures whose styles had something old and something new, such as the tenor saxophonists Dick Wilson and Henry Bridges Jr., were made welcome; the trumpeter Peanuts Holland and the pianist Clyde Hart were other regular visitors. One figure bridged both styles and achieved a substantial reputation as a pianist, composer and arranger; this was Tadd Dameron.

Other important visitors were the tenor saxophonist Lester Young, the master of the jam session Art Tatum, and the guitarist

Pianist, composer and arranger Tadd Dameron.

Charlie Christian. Much of Christian's most innovative solo work took place at Minton's: he effectively changed the function of the guitar by adopting the electric instrument and developing it from a rhythm instrument into a member of the front line. No longer acoustic and quiet, but amplified and loud, it could compete with saxophones and brass.

Art Tatum 'master of the jam session' a decade or so later than the days at Minton's with other musicians.

In addition to Christian, the trumpeter Dizzy Gillespie was soon a frequent visitor. Gillespie had been a member of Teddy Hill's band in 1937, including going on a tour to Europe. He then joined Cab Calloway's big band in 1939, and it was while on tour with Cab in the 1940s that he met Charlie Parker in Kansas City. His first experiments with bop date from around this time. Despite a superficial tendency to play-act, Gillespie was a dedicated, serious musician, playing as often as he could and anywhere he could. Dizzy's favourite trumpeter was the swing musician Roy Eldridge but, whereas perhaps musicians of the older generation were more concerned with intonation and tone, Gillespie sought to explore new harmonics and to extend the range of his instrument beyond anything previously attempted, as well as to improve the dexterity with which phrases could be executed. One night, after weeks of trying, Gillespie cut the old master Eldridge. This was perhaps only one night out of many, but it was a turning point. Afterwards the younger musicians began to close ranks against the older swing players. However, Eldridge, and many of the others, never stopped coming to the club. Gillespie's work survives on private recordings made at Minton's. Some (including *Kerouac*, 1941) have now been issued, and display his emerging grasp of a new solo trumpet style. The writer Thomas Owens has pointed out Gillespie's ability by 1942 to take a fully-formed bop solo in a big-band context, such as Lucky Millinder's *Big John Special*. In many respects this parallels the solo voice which Bud Powell was to develop in 1943–4 with Cootie Williams.

It was into the atmosphere of Minton's that Monk brought the adolescent Bud Powell. In a sleeve note by the writer Grover Sales, Monk is quoted as saying, 'I brought Bud Powell round when he first started – that's never been in print: I'm the only one he really digs.'

Powell was not accepted at first by the other musicians, probably because at that time his ability didn't meet with their high standards. However, Monk insisted that he be recognised and allowed to continue to play. Powell's case was not helped when, on his first visit, he put his feet up on the table on the fresh white tablecloth. Monk intervened with the waiter who was about to throw the younger man out, making excuses for him and asking that he be allowed to stay because he had talent. Monk said later that he was the only one to understand what Powell was playing; even Powell himself didn't know the advanced chords or understand the new harmonies. Monk said, 'He wasn't playing much then . . . I was the only one who dug him.' There was certainly, even then, a close rapport between the two men. Kenny Clarke recalled: 'Monk wrote for Bud. All his music was written for Bud Powell. All his piano music, he deliberately wrote for Bud just like a composer writes for a singer. When you hear Bud play Monk's music, then you really hear something.'

There was a chance that Bud might have become a major figure on 52nd Street earlier than he actually did. In 1943, while he was still with Cootie Williams, Dizzy Gillespie and Oscar Pettiford approached Powell to join them in a group which also included Max Roach, Don Byas and Charlie Parker. According to the pianist Billy Taylor, 'Cootie was [Bud's] guardian and wouldn't let him go. So the band opened without a piano.' The piano chair was eventually taken by George Wallington, whom Gillespie has described as having a style based on Powell's.

Still, on his night off from Williams, Powell would head for Minton's or for Clark Monroe's Uptown House, where the bop pioneers gathered after hours. During the 1943–5 period with Cootie, Bud was never a member of the house band at any of these clubs. This is confirmed by Gillespie in his autobiography: 'Bud Powell never played at Minton's' (by which he means 'played' in the sense of being a regular band member). Gillespie was close to Powell in the early 1940s, and told Leonard Feather that Powell was amongst those musicians who would gather at Dizzy's apartment or at Dewey Square, with such others as Benny Harris and Freddie Webster, to discuss the new music long into the night.

We have already seen that Al Tinney and others observed Powell's occasional bursts of pugnacious or violent behaviour in the mid-1940s. From his early days at Minton's, the introverted Powell was noted for behaviour which was not so much violent as strange or odd. He was known as the 'quiet one' or the 'strange one'. Some have suggested that this began as a cover for shyness and was used as a form of self-defence, but there is no doubt that it was also a way of attracting attention.

Elmo Hope was to tell Dexter Gordon that it was he who introduced Powell to the ruse of acting crazy. But Thelonious Monk told Jules Colomby, the brother of Monk's manager, that Powell started acting that way after suggestions from Monk.

The blind pianist Lennie Tristano told Robert Reisner of an incident when he was in the company of Charlie Parker. 'I was sitting with Charlie and some musicians at a table in Birdland when Bud Powell came by and said hello, then for no apparent reason, he said, "You know, Bird, you ain't shit. You don't kill me. You ain't playing shit now," and went on putting him down unmercifully. I said, "Bud, don't talk that way: Bird's your poppa."

'Bird said, "Lennie, don't pay any attention. I dig the way he plays . . . You think he is crazy? I taught him to act that way."'

Dexter Gordon was to remember Powell as always having been on the border line. 'Because he'd go off into things – expressions, telltale things that would let you know he was off.' Al Tinney, as we know, had been asked by Bud's mother to look after him, as Powell was liable to drink too much. In Tinney's phrase, Powell was 'a little bit on the alcohol'. But it was quite clearly not alcohol alone, nor suggestions from other musicians, that led to Powell's oddness. The signs of incipient mental illness were, in retrospect, all too obvious. As the 1940s went on his behaviour grew worse and more erratic.

If a turning-point were needed, a single and highly significant incident has generally been regarded as having tipped Powell over the boundaries of sanity. In 1945 he began to get into trouble with the law. Early that year he was arrested for the first time. He had been drinking and became very noisy in Philadelphia's Broad Street station. He was charged with disorderly conduct. Several musicians reckon he was beaten over the head by the police so badly he was for ever afterwards mentally damaged. This physical damage is believed by many to be the beginning of all his problems.

At the time of his arrest in 1945, Powell was still playing with Cootie Williams. Williams said: 'He was a genius. But he got into trouble while he was with me and got hurt. This was the first time he went into the sanitorium. We went to play a job in Philly and he was a little late. And high when he got there. So he didn't come back with us that night when we finished work. The next day the FBI called and told me they had him in jail. I gave them his mother's phone number. She found they'd beaten him so badly around the head that she had to go get him. She couldn't bring him back on the train and had to hire a car. His head was so damaged he ended in Bellevue; his sickness started right there.'

It is unlikely that the FBI were involved. Williams was almost certainly contacted by the Philadelphia police since he was, after all, Bud's legal guardian. A request for disclosure of Powell's FBI record under the Freedom of Information Act, as part of the preparation of this book, yielded 'no record responsive to your request . . . pertaining to Earl "Bud" Powell.'

Max Roach, an early friend of Powell's, was later to claim that Powell had suffered brain damage at that time. 'When they saw black men congregating in groups of more than three or four or five the police would say, "Okay, break it up." Bud took issue with them and they beat him to the ground.' Roach's claim came at a period when he was active in politics, adopting the Black Power theme of the 1960s. He said Powell's arrest occurred when there was serious rioting in Harlem and elsewhere as Blacks protested about segregation in the US army and navy.

Powell was fined before he was released into his mother's care. He went to his mother's house at Willow Grove, Pennsylvania, to rest and recover, but a month later he was sent to Pilgrim State Hospital, a mental institution on Long Island. He was to remain there for ten months. At Pilgrim State he talked garrulously throughout his stay to anyone who would listen. He was considered to be over-active, his thoughts flying away with him.

Further, and somewhat contradictory, information about this event appears in *La Danse des Infidèles*. Francis Paudras dates Bud's assault by police as 21 January 1945. He suggests that it happened in a club near Philadelphia where Bud had gone (after his job with Cootie) to hear Monk, in a group which also included

Max Roach. As the musicians packed up, a hint of marijuana in the air, the club was raided by the police. Powell was struck trying to prevent Monk from being arrested.

The accounts agree in that Paudras relates Powell's discharge from the custody of the police to that of his mother, but he suggests that (after superficial dressing of his head wound in hospital) Powell was imprisoned in Philadelphia and subjected to dousing in ammoniac water to 'calm him down'. His mother, Pearl, collected him, and cared for him with the help of an eighteen-year-old girl, Frances Barnes, who had been friendly with Bud for a couple of years. Bud took up his musical life again, but Paudras says he suffered from persistent headaches, and was placed under medical observation, being referred to the Creedmore Hospital, where he spent thirteen months.

Paudras has almost certainly conjoined two separate incidents, since it is relatively clear Powell was first at Pilgrim State, and we know that he was working again long before thirteen months were up.

When Bud eventually came out of hospital he had a busy year recording and playing on 52nd Street, from October 1945 through 1946 to early 1947. Virtually the first job he had was playing at the Three Deuces with the quintet formed by Dizzy Gillespie after the break-up of his first big band in late 1945. The band included Curly Russell, Max Roach and – at the height of his powers – Charlie Parker. Gillespie recalled: 'Bud Powell was the definitive pianist of the bebop era. He fitted in with us more than anybody else because of the fluidity of his phrasing. He played just like we did, more than anybody else.'

The band changed when Roach was replaced by Stan Levey and Russell by Ray Brown. According to Brown, Roach was still in the band when he joined, and the main attribute he needed was stamina. 'They liked to play fast . . . it didn't bother me to play fast . . . it was just a matter of learning the way they played changes. Because Dizzy played, he voiced his chords differently, and he wanted a different bassist.'

Soon, Milt Jackson joined on vibes. Brown remembered: 'Everybody in that band did something in the music business, there was no question about it. Bud and Max and Milt and I were the youngest guys. Dizzy and Bird were a little older than us.'

The Parker–Gillespie Quintet had effectively broken up by late October 1945, when Parker opened at the Three Deuces fronting his own group with Miles Davis, Al Haig, Curly Russell and Stan Levey. In early November 1945 a number of clubs, including the

Spotlite, were closed down by the police. Some remained closed for a number of weeks.

On 26 November, Parker, Davis, Russell and Max Roach went into the studio to record a session for Savoy. Accounts vary over what was intended – but what eventually happened was that Gillespie played piano behind Davis's trumpet, and, when Dizzy took over trumpet himself on *Ko-Ko*, Argonne Thornton (Sadik Hakim) came to the keyboard. Powell had originally been booked for the session, but the producer, Teddy Reig, recalls that Bud had gone home to his mother in Philadelphia. Owing to Union difficulties, Thornton was listed on the labels as Hen Gates, fuelling a lengthy controversy that the pianist was either Monk or Powell. It is now generally accepted that Powell did not appear on this session.

Max Roach, early 1946, nicknamed 'Tojo' by Charlie Parker.

The young, bespectacled Max Roach, nicknamed Tojo by Parker owing to his thick hornrimmed glasses, was asked back to join Gillespie's next big band. Powell was also to be a member. The band rehearsed in early 1946 at the Spotlite (owned by Clark Monroe, who also ran the musicians' hangout the Uptown House) and was based on Gillespie's new quintet, which included Milt Jackson, Ray Brown and Sonny Stitt.

Bud Powell did not last long. Gillespie said: 'The money was a little erratic, and Bud was super erratic, and I had to do something about that, so I got Monk.' Powell returned to the clubs and odd sessions of 52nd Street.

Amongst the musical high-points of this year of activity on The Street are two groups of recordings from August and September 1946 with the Be-Bop Boys. These have a number of the most influential bop musicians included in the band, among them Kenny Dorham, Sonny Stitt and Kenny Clarke. The 5 September sides were made under Clarke's leadership, and contain neat, uncluttered arrangements. The following day, less structured pieces with looser charts led to a more edgy and nervous session.

The ideal balance between the formality of the first September session and the loose, frenetic qualities of the second was achieved on the August date. Singer Dave Lambert is quoted in Jim Burns's essay on these sides (for *Jazz Journal* in October 1969) as saying that the tunes exemplify precisely the Minton's attitude of frightening off musicians of a low standard: 'The terrific tempos, the keys that no one ordinarily played in, just created a situation like Haydn's *Farewell Symphony*, only in up tempo. The musicians petered off, and the men were separated from the boys. One of the very fast tunes sometimes played for this weeding-out process was written by Bud Powell and was a variation of *Cherokee*. The number was aptly titled *Serenade For Squares*.' This tune appears as *Serenade To A Square* on the August recording date.

In May 1947 Powell started to drink heavily again. He was abusive when drunk, and once more began to get into brawls, which soon gained him a bad reputation. He also developed an irrational fear of being attacked when out on the street.

There is some evidence that Powell was disturbed by his colour and the prejudice his race attracted. He was once seen at Birdland obsessively rubbing his hands to remove the colour, and yet he was to tell Miles Davis that he wished he had a blacker skin, that he was as black as Davis himself.

Several writers have suggested that, although he had a sense of personal inferiority caused by his colour, his sense of inferiority about his music was a greater cause of discomfort and that this was fundamental in triggering his collapses. Some have said this feeling came from the fact that audiences had not responded to him in the early part of his career. The pianist Marian McPartland said as much when she suggested that greater audience appreciation in his earlier years would have been his salvation. Altoist Jackie McLean said the same when he suggested that, if Powell could have been handled earlier by Alfred Lion and Francis Wolff, he would have turned into a much different person. Lion and Wolff were the men behind the Blue Note label, for which Powell recorded several times, mainly in the 1950s. They were two good friends who treated Powell with the greatest respect. It is hard to understand exactly what McPartland and McLean meant by their reference to earlier years and audience appreciation. Powell struggled a little at first, but rapidly made his name as the best piano player of his generation. By 1949 he had already cut his first records for Blue Note.

In April 1947, Charlie Parker had returned to New York after rehabilitation on the West Coast at Camarillo State Hospital. Fit and relaxed, Bird told Leonard Feather that he was hoping to persuade Bud Powell to join him on a lengthy vacation on a Pennsylvania farm, to escape the pressures of 52nd Street. Powell did not go; instead he suffered another breakdown, a complete collapse, in November 1947. He was re-committed, this time to Creedmore, where he stayed eleven months. While there he was subjected to electric shock treatment but little improvement was noted. He was allowed to play occasionally in the hospital, but only under supervision.

CHAPTER 3

REHABILITATION – THE GREAT YEARS

At the beginning of 1947, eleven months before he collapsed, Powell had recorded perhaps the finest demonstrations of his early prowess. Eventually issued on the Roost label, the playing on such tracks as *Indiana* and *Bud's Bubble* shows Powell's extraordinary dexterity. It is clear from these why his contemporaries held him in such high regard. Al Haig, for instance, is quoted by Ira Gitler as saying: 'Bud's playing was so completely perfect and so highly stylized in that idiom. He outbirded Bird and he outdizzied Dizzy. And here he was, playing on a percussive instrument . . . not a front line instrument, and at times outdoing any of them.'

There is considerable evidence that the electric shock treatment Powell received destroyed much of his memory. He found himself caught up in the bizarre, booming business of psychiatric care during the years following World War II. Before the war, most US psychiatric wards were staffed by two attendants, who lived in. The wards often provided homes for those who otherwise could not afford one, and a range of disturbed and difficult people were cared for. The draft and well-paid defence work attracted experienced staff away during the war, while doctors also went into the services, or into private practice. As hospitals learnt to cope with skeleton staffs, and some inmates were co-opted to deal with other, more complex, patients, the tax-supported institutions showed signs of being unable to cope. There was growing overcrowding, an unbearable and unmanageable workload and, inevitably, decay and abuse. At the same time, however, the after-effects of the war threw more patients than ever into full-time psychiatric care.

An examination of the literature which deals with these institutions is harrowing. Charlie Parker narrowly avoided a lobotomy – the treatment developed by the Portuguese neurologist Egas Moniz which involved severing certain portions of the brain to bring about radical changes in behaviour. The film actress

Frances Farmer was less fortunate, and her biographer, William Arnold, believes she underwent this operation.

Electric shock treatment, which involved the passing of 70/130 volts through a patient's temples for between $\frac{1}{10}$th and $\frac{5}{10}$ths of a second, was a standard treatment for schizophrenia. Powell, with his reputation for pugnacious behaviour and awkwardness, would have been an obvious candidate for such treatment. Gradually the aggressive young man became cowed and introspective, with a dislike of going far from home and, as time went on, growing self-doubts about his playing.

Marian McPartland and Elmo Hope both visited him in hospital. Hope reported that, denied regular access to a piano, Powell had drawn a keyboard on the walls of his cell. Bud would finger chords on these keys and ask his visitors what they thought of the sounds. Over the weeks, Bud's visitors began to notice a gradual physical degeneration. Eventually, Hope encountered a young doctor who had heard of Powell and who took charge of his case: sedatives were discontinued, the shock treatments abated, and when supervised (as mentioned in the preceding chapter) Bud was allowed to play the hospital's ailing upright piano, with its several inoperative notes. As Bud began to recover, he asked Marian McPartland if the outside world had forgotten him.

The irony of this is that, beyond the clubs of New York, and apart from a few isolated recordings, the outside world had barely yet discovered him. The 10 January 1947 sessions had not been issued, and all Bud's other recordings involved ensembles larger than piano trios. Consequently, with the exception of the Roost sides, all that we know of Powell as a solo pianist dates from after this period in Creedmore.

Eventually allowed out, after an adjustment period of weekend leaves, Powell stayed at the family home on St Nicholas Avenue in Harlem, between 140th and 141st streets. It was here that the altoist Jackie McLean was taken to meet Bud, after a chance encounter with Richie Powell in the record shop run by McLean's stepfather, Jimmy Briggs.

'Two large French doors opened and: "My brother tells me you don't believe that I'm Bud Powell." And so, being sixteen years old and inquisitive I said, "Well, like I said, I never saw Bud Powell. I only know Bud Powell by music, you know." Very arrogant, like I knew I was into something. With this, Bud went to the piano and sat down; and there was no question. It was Bud.'

The bearded Powell was quiet, eccentric, but – where the young McLean was concerned – nonetheless friendly. When McLean transgressed the unwritten law by bringing an uninvited guest into Powell's house, the visitor was quickly ejected with the words

Jackie McLean at the time of his encounter with Bud Powell.

'Never darken the portals of my abode again!' Bud displayed a fondness for odd turns of phrase, and would deliver them for maximum dramatic effect. Jackie accompanied Bud to some of his regular gigs: the Royal Roost, for instance, at 1674 Broadway (on West 47th Street), with its curious stage decorated in large artificial leaves; or the Clique (which later became Birdland), at 1618 Broadway (at 52nd Street). McLean also saw Bud attending an afternoon ballroom job, where he followed the British pianist George Shearing onto the stage. Bud 'collared' Shearing, saying, 'How dare you play before me?' Shearing reacted calmly, and Bud was suddenly overcome with remorse in the middle of his set, walking offstage briefly to confront McLean with: 'Jackie, I collared a blind man . . .' and a look of intense concern.

During late 1948 and 1949, when McLean was friendly with Bud, several accounts suggest that Powell was married, and in early 1949 a daughter, Celia, was born. After recording a number dedicated to her for Norman Granz's Clef label in May 1949, Bud was apparently re-committed to Creedmore. It was small consolation that 'his playing was one of the highlights of the hospital's annual minstrel show'. He was back in the outside world by August, however, when he made his first session for Blue Note, the label run by Alfred Lion and Francis Wolff.

At home during this period, Bud was quiet, saying little, perhaps laughing quietly to himself, getting up to eat or play the piano. Friends remember that he was already starting to be silent in the company of strangers, and, from time to time, when the names of fellow musicians were mentioned, Powell asked about them as if they were strangers. He also had to be told about events in which he had participated and what he had done. By all accounts his actual musical memory was still unimpaired at this point, but a decade later, in Paris, Francis Paudras remembers Bud's incredulity at hearing his own records, and that he could not identify the sound of his own playing.

Immediately after the war, the place to hear jazz in New York was on 52nd Street, between Fifth Avenue and Broadway. Many small clubs had sprung up during the war years, taking over empty basements or unused ground floors. By day the area looked dingy – a decaying collection of run-down four storey buildings – but after dark the neon lights of the clubs and their brightly lit marquees transformed the street into a fairyland of jazz, where patrons could stroll from club to club and hear almost all jazz styles played by legendary figures of the music.

'The Street', as it became known, was home to a number of clubs which moved from one address to another, so there are conflicting accounts of which club was where. As far as can be ascertained, between 1946 and 1948 the configuration of the Street was something like this:

18 West 52nd Street:	Club 18 (later the Troubadour)
38 West 52nd Street:	the Flamingo
53 West 52nd Street:	Jimmy Ryan's
56 West 52nd Street:	Spotlite (later the Famous Door)
57 West 52nd Street:	Onyx Club (previously at 35, 62 and 72 West 52nd)
62 West 52nd Street:	Samoa (formerly the Onyx)
66 West 52nd Street:	Downbeat (formerly the Yacht Club)
72 West 52nd Street:	Three Deuces (formerly the Onyx)
137 West 52nd Street:	Kelly's Stable
144 West 52nd Street:	Hickory House.

There is a good account of the Street at night in the auto-biography of Bob Wilber, who started to visit the clubs there at precisely the period of Powell's rehabilitation. Wilber recalls one evening in which he heard Zutty Singleton's trio at Ryan's, Billie

The picture of Powell from the mid 1950s used on the album cover of the Sonny Stitt session described on page 46.

Holiday with the Al Casey Trio at the Onyx, and Coleman Hawkins at Kelly's Stable. 'The excitement and glamor of the Street at night was something else . . .'

Wilber and his teenage friends who made the journey into the city from the northern suburb of Scarsdale were allowed into the clubs underage, and on condition they avoided alcohol. Regular patrons were not so lucky. Most of the venues were small and overpriced; 75 cents was the charge for beer or a diluted whisky, and there was usually a cover charge of about $3.00. The managements would often operate a policy of clearing the club between each thirty-minute set, or making an additional cover charge.

The 52nd Street clubs steadily declined after about 1947. The high cost of living, the post-war recession, and the desire of the police department to clean up the area gradually closed the doors of the clubs. Some became strip joints – others were cleared to make way for building developments.

By the 1950s, the jazz scene had moved to Broadway. The Royal Roost set the precedent for a more lavish style of club than those of the Street. Apart from the Roost, there were:

Basin Street (at Broadway and West 51st Street)
Bop City (at 1619 Broadway and West 49th)
Ebony (1618 Broadway, which became the Clique, and then Birdland)
Zanzibar (at Broadway and West 49th).

During the period from 1947 to 1950, Powell was active in many of these clubs, both those on the Street and those which opened later on Broadway. He played for Don Byas, Sid Catlett, Dexter Gordon, John Kirby, J. J. Johnson and Allan Eager as well as his own trio.

Despite Powell's withdrawn character in terms of his domestic life at this time, both before and after his 1947–8 breakdown he was able to summon up remarkable musical performances. He established a highly individual stage persona, which changed little in terms of his playing stance and attitude throughout the remainder of his career. He would generally sit slightly sideways at the keyboard (a trait which became more evident during the Paris years on account of his increasing girth). His right leg would be twisted out, his foot stabbing the floor. His trouser legs had a tendency to ride up over his calves, and he would hunch his shoulders, giving a sense to the onlooker of his great physical involvement in the music.

The other characteristic (which became more pronounced over the years, as witness Paudras's description of Powell's first Parisian visit in Chapter Five) was the gutteral grunting and heavy breathing which accompanied his playing. This can be heard on many of his recordings from all periods, and a sense of the facial mannerisms which went with this can be gleaned from photographs which show his upper lip drawn high over his front teeth, and his features contorted. It is interesting to note the parallels here between Powell and the Canadian classical pianist Glenn Gould, who displayed a similar physical involvement in his playing, and whose grunting and singing can be heard on many of his recordings.

There are many accounts of Powell's devastating playing during these years. Ira Gitler, in *Jazz Masters of the Forties*, tells of a night at the Three Deuces in mid-1947. Powell and Fats Navarro came into the club whilst Charlie Parker's quintet was on the stand. They sat in for a set in place of Miles Davis and Duke Jordan, and launched into the familiar signature tune of many boppers of the period, Monk's *52nd Street Theme*. At breakneck speed, Powell's playing eclipsed that of Parker and Navarro: 'For twenty or twenty-five choruses, he hung the audience on its nerve ends, playing music of demonically driven beauty, music of hard, unflinching swing, music of genius.'

At the end of the following year, Powell was part of an all-star bop amalgam under the general direction of Oscar Pettiford. This appears to be the band that shows up in the discography as broadcasting from the Royal Roost on 19 December 1948, although most published accounts suggest that the group played at the Clique. Amongst the sidemen at the Clique were Miles Davis, Fats Navarro, Lucky Thompson, Dexter Gordon, Kai Winding, Milt Jackson and Kenny Clarke, as well as Powell and Pettiford. The rhythm section was to be reunited in Paris many years later, but Pettiford's recollections of the 1948 band were tinged with disappointment according to Marshall Stearns, who quotes the bassist's unhappiness with the fact that each forty-five-minute set was an excuse for another extended solo, and not for the band to work as a whole: 'One or two members soloed, and the rest walked off the stand . . . nobody bothered about the audience.'

Other recollections of this group suggest that whenever Powell took a solo the members of the front line who were on stage turned to face the pianist. One night he took a 'particularly great' solo, and then got up and walked off the stand, feeling there was nothing more to be said, and applauding himself as he went. Jackson had to switch to piano to finish the number. Powell could still display great self confidence in his own playing at this stage, and was certain of his own worth and ability.

Art Tatum, who was in many respects Powell's lifelong idol, confirmed Bud's status. During 1950, Powell was booked opposite

Tatum at Birdland. The younger man told Tatum after one of his sets that he had made five mistakes in a Chopin prelude. Heatedly, Tatum replied that Powell was just a right-hand piano player, and had no left hand to speak of, whilst he, Tatum, had a whole rhythm section in his left hand. For the first number the next night, Powell played *Sometimes I'm Happy* at a rapid-fire tempo entirely with his left hand. Tatum hardly knew how to react, and after the set he told a friend: 'Don't tell the kid I said it, but . . . I was wrong. He's got one hell of a left hand.' The friend did tell Powell, to his immense pleasure. Even in the Parisian days, Francis Paudras tells us that Powell maintained a great admiration for Tatum, always preferring to listen to Tatum's records. In many of Powell's later ballad performances he adopts a style redolent of Tatum's; at times the two men's work is almost indistinguishable.

Charting Powell's associations accurately between his emergence from hospital and his next period of illness in the early 1950s is complex. In 1948 we know he was in Miles Davis's band at

Miles Davis, 1949, with Milt Jackson (vibes) and Bud Powell.

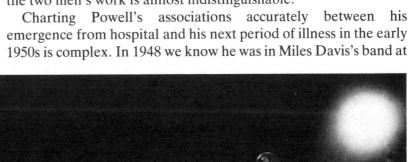

the Royal Roost. He broadcast from the Roost in late 1948, and, if we believe the sources referred to above, also worked at the Clique. This club ran from late 1948 until around July 1949, and Bud was there on and off with Davis's quintet. Bud recorded for Norman Granz with Ray Brown and Max Roach (both former associates from his abortive stay with Gillespie's big band) in May 1949, going on to record his own first session for Blue Note in August, with Fats Navarro and Sonny Rollins.

In December 1949, Powell recorded with Sonny Stitt's quartet for Prestige (there is more information below concerning this session). He then took part in Leonard Feather's third annual Christmas jazz concert from Carnegie Hall, an event which was taped by Voice of America and issued privately by a collectors' organisation. For this, which involved Sonny Stitt and Miles Davis, Bud was teamed with bassist Curly Russell and Max Roach, a rhythm section which recorded as a trio a few days later for Norman Granz.

Stitt's quartet made a second session for Prestige a week or two later in January 1950, shortly before Powell took a regular job with the Stan Getz–Miles Davis Sextet. (For this group's broadcast, recorded by Boris Rose from a Birdland session on 10 February, Powell was unfortunately replaced by Tadd Dameron, hence losing the opportunity to preserve the work of this cooperative for posterity.) The band apparently (according to Jack Chambers, Davis's biographer) lasted for some weeks, although Davis returned to the studios in March to record with his nonet, involving only one or two of the sidemen from the regular band.

The Powell–Davis association continued later in 1950, however, as Davis led what turned out to be virtually the last of his straightforward bop bands at the Orchid, also involving Stitt and Wardell Gray.

In Chambers's *Milestones*, he quotes singer Babs Gonzales as suggesting that Davis and Powell were 'strung out and in hock to' the 52nd Street club owners. Although Chambers presents evidence of Davis's addiction, there is no confirmatory evidence that Powell was a heroin addict. Paudras points out that Powell was arrested in June 1951 for drug trafficking, but this appears to have been a rather clumsy attempt to plant marijuana on the mentally-ill pianist by a teenage informer called Lynn Messier.

There are signs that, despite Powell's quiet home life in Harlem, his friendship with McLean and his remarkable powers at the keyboard, he was still not a well man. The story of his 1949 and 1950 recordings with Stitt's quartet backs up this view. Stitt kept goading Powell with remarks which addressed him sarcastically as 'the great Bud Powell'. Powell reacted with a burst of his former

Jackie McLean – a later shot of Powell's friend and associate.

belligerence. Possibly this is what Stitt had intended, since Powell's searching, aggressive playing, particularly on *All God's Chillun*, is angrily brilliant. The aggression continued, apparently, when Powell shouted to Bob Weinstock, the president of Prestige: 'Hey Fats, go out and get us some sandwiches.'

Powell's behaviour on the bandstand also changed. He would face his audience with a fixed stare between numbers, or when other musicians took a solo. He would hold the stare, or a grimace, for minutes at a time. While this might be seen as comparable with the attitude of contempt for an audience described by Pettiford in the context of the Clique sessions, viewed as part of a general deterioration of Powell's spirit it clearly shows an aspect of his return to an unstable condition.

In mid-1951, Powell started to drink heavily again, and several sources report that he was arrested. This is almost certainly the arrest for drug trafficking in June. In May, he had worked (according to *Jazz Hot*) with Parker and Gillespie at Birdland. The next account of him in that magazine, from October, reports that once more he was in an asylum.

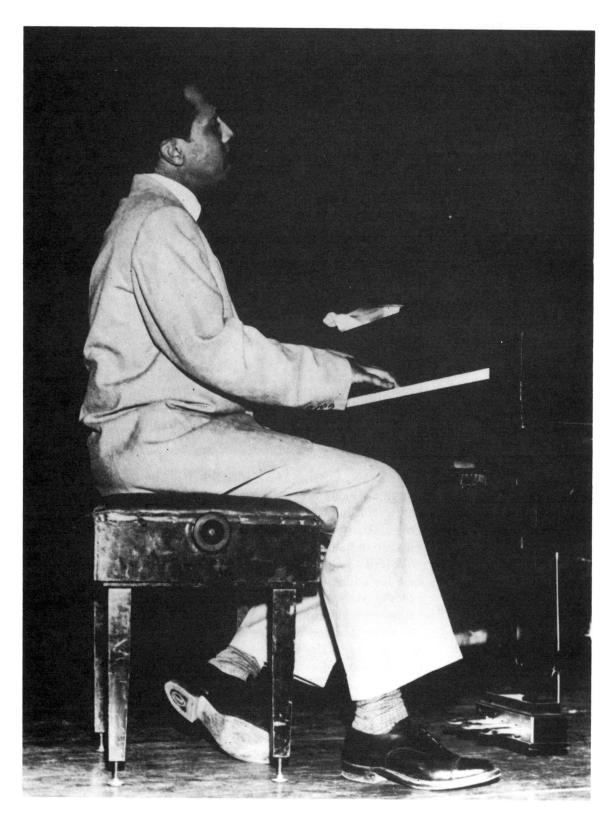

In the period following his arrest, Powell had apparently been put in the Tombs prison, where he went berserk, shouting hysterically that people were trying to kill him. As in his earlier period of imprisonment, he was drenched with buckets of ammoniated water. Following a by now familiar pattern, he was transferred to the Bellevue and ultimately to Pilgrim State.

The great years were almost over. What survives from 1947 to 1951 is some of Powell's finest playing, and we are fortunate that only shortly before he disappeared from the recording studios for almost two years Powell made a session for Blue Note, in May 1951. The intense reworking of *Un Poco Loco* shows his ability to channel mental energy into his work, and his dexterity and ideas are on a par with those exhibited in the Roost recordings of the beginning of the period. It is on his work from these years that Powell's reputation rests, and on this that he should be judged in comparison with other pianists, unhampered by his health and mental trouble.

CHAPTER 4

THE MID 1950s – NEW YORK

From 4 September 1952, Powell had been committed in the Pilgrim State mental institution. It is probable that he underwent intensive electric shock treatment once more, as he had done in 1949. He was allowed to play the piano, but only once a week, under supervision. The attendant stopped the session if Powell was made too agitated by his music.

In December 1952, shortly before being released, Powell was permitted two one-night passes. These were obtained for him by Oscar Goodstein, the manager of Birdland, to see how he would cope with what was his anticipated working environment. He handled it well, and was released, to start a residency at Birdland. He was watched closely and denied alcohol. Instead of strong liquids, he would drink ten to twenty cokes or ginger ales and several double-egg malteds in the course of a night's session. This is entirely consistent with Francis Paudras's account of the Paris years, during which he observed that Powell's metabolism demanded that he intake large and frequent quantities of fluid. With the success of these experiments, Powell transferred once more to Creedmore.

On 5 February 1953, Powell was released into the custody of Oscar Goodstein, who became his agent, manager, and – effectively – guardian. Two days later, on 7 February, Powell began to broadcast from the Royal Roost in New York. On and off, he continued to play regularly on the radio throughout the year. It is possible to piece together a fairly accurate account of his working associations over the twelve months by comparing what survives from the airshot recordings that remain. More importantly, it is possible to hear in his playing the changes it underwent through perhaps the most regular aural documentation of any stage in his career.

In February, the trio consisted of Oscar Pettiford on bass and

A mid-1950s photograph of Bud Powell used by Blue Note Records for alternate takes from most of their recording sessions with Powell from 1949-1963.

Roy Haynes on drums. The following month, for the first two weeks, Powell was teamed with Franklin Skeete on bass and Sonny Payne on drums. Frank Skeete was a session bassist who made numerous recordings during the 1940s and 1950s with swing and bop musicians, including Eddie 'Lockjaw' Davis, Harold 'Shorty' Baker and the tenor saxophonist Joe Holiday. Sonny Payne, the son of drummer Chris Columbus, was to go on to become Count Basie's drummer for many years. By mid-March, these two musicians had been replaced by more familiar company, and Haynes returned to the drum chair, while Charles Mingus took over on bass.

According to Oscar Goodstein, on 9 March 1953, Powell got married, to a white woman, Audrey Hill. The marriage did not

Charles Mingus, bassist in Powell's trio from March 1953.

last, and by the mid-1960s Audrey Hill Powell was living in California. The marriage does not seem to have disrupted the regular work and broadcasts of Powell, Mingus and Haynes.

Early in April, the trio was in Washington, and most of a complete evening at the Club Kavakos survives on Elektra Musician E1-60030, a session recorded by the collector Bill Potts. Mingus is under-recorded, and although his bass lines appear to match Powell's left-hand patterns, in a manner quite unlike the familiar walking-bass playing of Tommy Potter or Curly Russell, it is hard to hear him. Haynes, by contrast, is much to the fore, and is in inspired form. He propels the trio with an authority and swing that launches Powell into some long, exciting linear improvisations. By contrast with Max Roach or Art Taylor on

A later photograph of Roy Haynes, drummer in the trio with Powell and Mingus (1953).

some of Powell's other sessions from this period, Haynes avoids the brushes and for many of the tracks uses sticks.

Powell's own playing is worthy of a number of observations, especially since this session was recorded only shortly before his famous appearance at Massey Hall in Toronto with the Quintet of the Year. There is no sign here of the attitude which was to prevail in his later years of playing at his best only in the concert hall, and leaving club jobs to run their course in a series of routine performances. He is in many ways more subtle and daring than at Massey Hall a few weeks later. On *Salt Peanuts* (which offers the opportunity for direct comparison) the Washington version is played at full tilt, with some breath-taking pianism in the solo lines. Haynes, who picks up Powell's left-hand punctuations and copies them on the bass drum or in left-hand snare accents, follows Powell's train of thought closely. The same synergy is at work in their renditions of a number of Gershwin and Shearing tunes. In Shearing's *Conception*, Powell experiments with tempo in a manner only possible with a drummer as firm and on form as Haynes. In both the first and last statements of the theme, Powell takes the 'channel' (the middle eight bars of the piece) and plays it almost out of time. Compared with his usual headlong rush, it is a very interesting effect, and creates a sensation of space normally achievable only by a pianist playing entirely solo.

Most noticeable of all is the concentration of intellectual energy into Powell's playing. Even when Mingus (normally a most interesting and compelling soloist) is soloing, the listener is drawn to the fill-ins and accompaniments played by Powell. Very few jazzmen had the ability to draw attention from other soloists by the quality of their accompaniments, but here Bud does it repeatedly, just as Louis Armstrong was so often to do behind Velma Middleton or Jewel Brown.

On the night of 15 May 1953, the New Jazz Society of Toronto presented their poll-winners' concert at Massey Hall. The resulting band, billed as the Quintet of the Year, consisted of Powell, Mingus and Max Roach (who played the first set as a trio), together with Charlie Parker and Dizzy Gillespie.

Because of an accident of planning, the concert coincided with the heavyweight boxing title fight between Rocky Marciano and Jersey Joe Walcott. Consequently, the 2500-seater hall was only about a quarter full. Photographs of the event show the quintet positioned at the front of a stage which was also set up for a local big band. It was plainly an expensive promotion for the local society, and one which did not recover its costs.

Mingus had contracted the quintet. Powell found that Goodstein had negotiated a high fee and top billing for him.

Dizzy Gillespie (seen here with Oscar Peterson, right) around the time of the Massey Hall concert.

Ironically, according to Brian Priestley, the street-wise Parker was the only one to be paid in full for the event, by securing cash from the box office, whilst the others contented themselves with cheques of dubious quality. In this, Priestley's account differs from Ross Russell's. In *Bird Lives*, Russell suggests that Parker, on discovering that the box-office receipts didn't cover the guarantee, obtained cheques from the organisers, drawn on their personal accounts. Russell also suggests that Powell was 'drunk from the first number onward', having 'just been released from a Long Island sanitarium after undergoing a long regime of electric shock treatments.' In fact, as we know, Powell had been out of Creedmore for over three months, and was working regularly. Like the other musicians, Powell no doubt repaired to the Brass Rail bar opposite the hall, but even if the alcohol had its usual effect on him of altering his behaviour, there is no real sign from the recording that Bud was not in control of his faculties as a pianist.

Mingus recorded the entire event for his Debut label, and

photographs show a single boom microphone placed directly in front of the concert grand piano, the cable snaking off from it in the direction of the bassist, who is rather uncomfortably poised behind Max Roach, and next to the unused drums belonging to the big band. Predictably, with this placing of the mike, both piano and bass are seriously under-recorded. Mingus, who was criticised for recording the event in the first place without plans to pay the musicians properly, attracted far more criticism for overdubbing his own parts afterwards in the studio. Brian Priestley's erudite account of this in his biography of Mingus points out that, on *All The Things You Are*, the bassist may be heard duetting with himself! He also recorded *Bass-ically Speaking* in the studio, with Billy Taylor taking Powell's place.

In the two following weeks, Parker was recorded at Birdland with Powell's trio, and recordings exist (surrounded by a considerable degree of uncertainty and speculation about exactly which airshots belong to which date) of Powell's work with his trio during June and July. Art Taylor became Powell's regular drummer and, when George Duvivier replaced Mingus in August, the trio was formed which Powell led for much of the 1950s.

Briefly, in September 1953, after the Duvivier–Taylor trio had recorded several times, Curly Russell rejoined the group for their weekly Birdland broadcasts. From September 1953 until June 1954, there are no commercially available recordings extant. During this time, Bud was booked for a concert and club tour of the West Coast. Henri Renaud reported in *Jazz Hot* for February 1954 that this would involve a twenty-week residency at the Haig in Los Angeles. Renaud (quoted in *La Danse des Infidèles*) says that, during Bud's Birdland residency in late 1953, he had told Oscar Goodstein that he thought he was playing badly. Between sets, Bud would sit silently and alone in a darkened corner of the club.

These difficulties were to continue to beset Powell on his tour. The bassist Curtis Counce, who had settled in Los Angeles in the mid-1940s, was paid extra to act as Powell's offstage companion, to guide him and keep him out of trouble. Observers reported that Bud was easily upset when in front of an audience, and was sometimes unable to play more than one solo at a performance. To many, this seemed to confirm his loss of self-belief, and the tour was cut short. Later in 1954 and again in 1955 he returned to hospital in Central Islip. He was allowed a piano in his room, and accounts suggest that he was as talkative in hospital as he was silent in the outside world.

In June 1954, Powell was well enough to record for Norman Granz, using a trio which once more included Art Taylor on drums, but with Percy Heath on bass. Between 1949 and 1951,

Powell had made some recordings for Granz, and in the mid-1950s he was contracted to Granz's Clef, Norgran and Verve labels, until a lawsuit (brought by Powell when tracks he was unhappy with were released) ended the agreement, although the action itself was unsuccessful.

Granz himself was taken with Bud's playing: 'It can be said in all sincerity and correctness that Bud Powell is one of the most talented and important figures to come along in jazz for a long time. A lot of his work is breathtaking; a lot of it is very touching and tasty. But, through it all Bud maintains the essential qualities of beat, drive and ideas . . .'

After another six-month gap, Granz recorded Powell again in December 1954 and January 1955. There are four sessions here, and the accompanists vary, including Percy Heath and Lloyd Trotman on bass, and Max Roach, Art Blakey and Kenny Clarke on drums. In a perceptive review of the recordings, Chris Sheridan (writing in *Jazz Journal International* in 1981) points out that these tracks display a growing stylistic similarity with Monk's playing. 'The commitment [to Monk] reflects an emotional attitude as much as an attempt to harness a withering technique. And, make no mistake, Bud's once-glittering dexterity was, by 1955, at best half-paced.'

One of the tracks Bud recorded in June 1954 was called *Buttercup*. It was named after Altevia Edwards, the woman who was to become his common-law wife, and who took over from Goodstein as Powell's manager. From the earliest days of their relationship, Buttercup, who had been a childhood friend of Powell's and who claimed friendship with many of the pioneers of bop, passed herself off as Powell's second wife. She told Kurt Mohr in 1958 that she had decided her destiny lay with Bud's when she found him in a mental hospital, locked in a solitary cell and confined in a straightjacket. 'His case was desperate. He didn't even recognise his own mother.' Apparently, though, he pleaded with his new visitor: 'Buttercup! Please! Untie me!'

She secured his release, and moved into an apartment with him on Long Island. They found a psychiatrist in whom Bud was able to confide, and with whom he made 'real progress'. But, to support his treatment, let alone Buttercup, Bud had to continue to work, despite his desperate mental state. She told Mohr that Bud talked freely with her in their apartment, although in company he was silent, not even having a sole friend in New York with whom he wished to converse.

It is almost certainly against this domestic background that Powell made his infamous final appearance with Parker at Birdland on 5 March 1955. Parker had earlier been banned from

the club for erratic behaviour, but this was to be his comeback, with Powell, Mingus, Kenny Dorham and Art Blakey.

Powell was almost certainly drunk as well as disturbed on this, the second of a two-night engagement. The evening before, he had tried to pick a quarrel with Bird, but the music had been reasonably successful. On the 5th, a Saturday, a big crowd had gathered to hear Parker et al, and Pee Wee Marquette, master of ceremonies (known as the 'Metre' of ceremonies on account of his diminutive stature), announced the band.

Mingus and Dorham came on stage, and were followed after a long pause by Powell. After several faltering dance steps, he sat at the piano and started to play *Little Willie Leaps*. Marcel Zannini, reporting for *Jazz Hot*, said: 'Bud wasn't capable of playing a single

Bud Powell with Buttercup

note . . . The tune was barely recognisable, and I couldn't believe my ears.' Mingus and Dorham attempted to cover for Bud, but he quickly turned his back on the piano at the end of a chorus, leaving just trumpet and bass. Hal Harewood, the drummer from J. J. Johnson's band, sat in on drums and attempted to fill the silences left by the piano.

Parker and Blakey appeared, Parker bolstered by the intake of several straight whiskies. Bird called a tune (Zannini reports this as *Hallucinations*, but Dorham remembered it as *Out Of Nowhere*). Powell launched, erratically, into *Little Willie Leaps*.

At this point accounts once more vary. Zannini, who had attended the session hoping to hear Powell, was bitterly disappointed. Parker signalled to Bud to stop, as Bud fought with both hands, and then one hand, to continue to keep time, before grinding to a halt. Mingus put his bass down. It was clear Bud was not going to play again, but he lingered, sitting at the piano. Blakey tried to cajole Powell, like a child, into playing. As Powell walked off the stage, Parker called Bud's name repeatedly, while Mingus attempted to disassociate himself from these 'sick people'. Dorham left the stage. Some customers left, others thought it was amusing: 'It was true that Saturday at Birdland no longer attracted real connoisseurs', said Zannini. 'Blakey, Parker and Mingus were the only ones to continue playing. This was the best moment of the evening. Their swelling volume, and the swing of these three "giants", filled the room, almost as if they were the Count Basie orchestra. The smiles came back to their lips: music won the day. Parker, his eyes closed, his face streaming with sweat, played his last choruses of blues magnificently. At the last moment, Bird proved that he was still the greatest.'

In many respects, this differs substantially from the versions of events in the standard biographies of Parker and Mingus. Zannini's account rings truer than Russell's, in which the crowd departs, leaving Parker alone on the stage; Bird then goes out into the night and finds a bar in which to drink several more whiskies, before returning, tearfully, to read his name in lights outside Birdland. Whatever the exact sequence of events, eight days later Parker was dead.

Powell, on the other hand, continued in his half-life with Buttercup, playing regularly, if erratically, at Birdland to meet his financial obligations. In April 1955 he recorded for Granz again, using the regular trio of Duvivier and Taylor.

'When you catch him right', recalled Duvivier, 'he can still do some surprising things. There have been times when Art Taylor and I would look at each other and say "*What?*" because of some way he conceived a tune. Those are the nights when his technique is clean, and his arpeggios aren't muffled. His eyes are clear; he becomes very aware; and he seems to be really enjoying himself. There have been times when he's been loose when he could take *Salt Peanuts*, let's say, at a fantastic tempo . . . and he'd sustain it. Other times he might start at that tempo but wouldn't be able to keep it up.'

For over a year after the April 1955 recordings, Bud did not appear in a studio. We know that in October 1955 he was working in Cleveland, in a trio with Mingus and the drummer Elvin Jones. This came about in a rather curious way. Jones told Whitney Balliett that he had been touring in a quartet with Mingus, Teddy Charles and the tenor saxophonist J. R. Monterose. Mingus and Charles argued constantly during a short tour to Newport, Toronto and Washington. Eventually, the bassist fired Jones from the band and then resigned himself, telling Jones, 'We'll go to Cleveland and play with Bud Powell.'

Eventually, at the end of October, Mingus left Powell to front his own band at the Café Bohemia in New York, and was replaced by Tommy Potter. Jones remembers this trio as working, on and off, for the next year and a half. 'Bud was very shaky, very sick,' recalled Jones, who went on to describe the familiar picture of the withdrawn, uncommunicative pianist. 'It ended up that I became the leader and was consulted about setting up and various routines. And during the day I'd visit with him and take him to the movies or on long walks. He would open up and be very rational.' The main problem was alcohol. If Bud took even a couple of drinks he went out of control, and Jones had to ration him severely. On the odd occasions when Bud got away, he was likely to go on a bender: '. . . once, when some people poured some wine into him . . . he was found the next morning in an alley in his underwear with even his shirt and tie stolen.' Jones remembers the trio finally broke up when Powell took off during the intermission at Birdland and didn't come back. The two men were not to meet again until shortly after Powell's return to New York from France in 1964, when he called in on Jones on his birthday, 'and brought me an autographed picture of himself as a present.'

Shortly after the Cleveland engagement, Francis Paudras, keeping an eye on the French press, noticed a report from Leonard Feather that Bud was back at Birdland: 'more on form than I've seen or heard him for a long time.' Nevertheless, Feather thought that Bud, who had put on weight, was less frenetic than he had been, and lacked the sparkling drive of his best early work.

Bud came to the attention of the press in March 1956, during an engagement at Newark, New Jersey, when he was jailed on a paternity suit filed by one Elvia Edwards. Powell was released on a

Powell about the time of his 1955 recordings for Norman Granz.

$5000 surety, and Oscar Goodstein testified on his behalf that electric shock treatment had rendered Powell sterile, therefore proving that Bud could not possibly be guilty. Almost certainly, 'Elvia' was Altevia Edwards, since the same year Buttercup produced a son, Johnny, whom she passed off for several years to come as Bud's child.

On 26 June 1956, Powell's younger brother Richie was killed. Richie was the regular pianist with the trumpeter Clifford Brown, a rising star, whose quintet (co-led with Max Roach) was one of the most influential bop groups of the era. Brown, Richie and Powell's wife were killed when their car skidded on the Pennsylvania Turnpike on the way home from a guest appearance with another band. It is generally assumed that this loss had a deep and lasting effect on Bud, but he was unwilling to be drawn on the subject in conversation, and what reactions it was possible to infer from his behaviour may very well be misleading.

In the fall of 1956, firmly under Buttercup's thumb, Bud made his last record for Granz and signed a new contract with Victor. In October, he recorded with his familiar trio of Duvivier and Taylor, producing an album for Victor called 'Strictly Powell'. In some respects, he was more fully in control of his playing than he had been since 1953, and he was contracted to tour Europe in a package show called 'Birdland '56'. In view of his mental state, it was probably somewhat irresponsible of his management to have agreed to the tour, but there is little doubt that it was lucrative for him at a time when his earning potential was not great.

As part of the package, Miles Davis and Lester Young appeared with a French rhythm section (René Urtreger, Pierre Michelot and Christian Garros), Bud played a solo set, and the concerts were wound up by the Modern Jazz Quartet. Many English fans travelled over to see the show, which played for two nights at the Salle Pleyel. Amongst them was Alun Morgan, who saw alarming evidence of Powell's declining abilities when the pianist attempted to sit in with Pierre Michelot and Al Levitt at the Club Saint-Germain. 'Someone said, "Bud's going to play," in a kind of shocked half-whisper . . . Bud went into a fast *Nice Work If You Can Get It* which began to degenerate into chaos before the end of the first chorus. A kind of paralysis seemed to have seized the pianist's hands and the more he tried to fight his way free, the more inaccurate became his fingering. Four choruses and it was over . . . Miles broke the tension by flinging a comforting arm round Bud's shoulders. "You know man, you shouldn't try to play when you're juiced like that."'

By electing to play his concert sets without bass and drums, Powell avoided the necessity to keep in with an ensemble. He

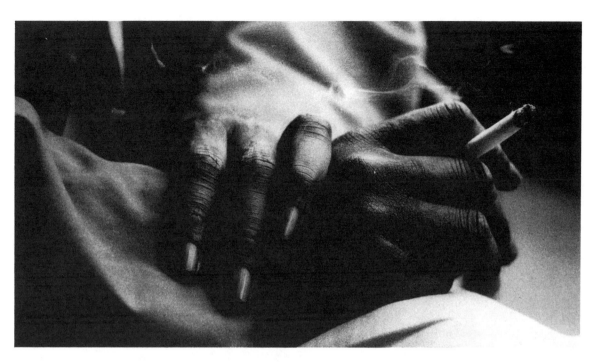

The hands of Bud Powell – photographed during his early visit to Paris.

could dictate his own time and play within his abilities. Mike Butcher, reviewing the concerts for *Jazz Journal*, wrote: 'He provided the controversial, least comfortable and . . . most shatteringly intense music of the night. The art of a mentally sick man who bares his soul for us to take or leave.'

Butcher goes on to describe Bud's jerky, mechanical walk, and his incoherent attempts to play *Hallelujah* and *I Want To Be Happy*. 'With *Cherokee* halfway through, however, Powell suddenly took command of his powers. He lunged into some dazzlingly percussive phrases, each more spine-chilling than the last. Then came an indescribably hypnotic transcription of *Over The Rainbow* . . . The agonised tension brought tears unashamedly to our eyes.' Interestingly, Powell kept close to the shape and routines of his recorded versions of the ballads, and on the second night he produced a set which, in that it avoided the extremes of his first, was lucid and controlled.

The European tour made enormous demands on Powell's stamina and stability, although (as will become clear in the next chapter) the medication which Buttercup administered to him to control his schizophrenia no doubt increased his tiredness and energy problems. Following reports of the 'Birdland '56' tour, Nat Hentoff, writing in *Down Beat* of 6 February 1957, asked if Powell might be able to receive 'continuous psychotherapy' whilst on tour. He pointed out that Powell followed up the European trip with a US tour with many members of the same package.

This prompted a reply from Maxwell Cohen, Powell's lawyer, in *Down Beat* of 6 March:

> Bud is no longer a judicial incompetent, nor for that matter is he a medical incompetent. Bud has been under constant treatment, and is under treatment from Dr Phillip Polatin, Associate Professor of Psychiatry, School of Physicians and Surgeons at Columbia University. He voluntarily visits Dr Polatin. There is a mutual regard and respect, and there has been a decisive improvement in Bud's health. Financially, although not constantly employed, he is in a better state now than for a number of years.
>
> What, then, is the explanation for what happened in Europe, and why must he be accompanied by someone on the Birdland tour?
>
> The adulation which the troupe received in Europe was excessive, and let us say candidly that all members of the troupe responded to the hospitality fluidly and flexibly. But the consequences of such hospitality were more prominently displayed by Bud. He cannot drink without a marked physical change in his appearance, walk and mannerisms . . . Bud is essentially a shy and withdrawn person and finds it difficult to decline invitations extended to him by fans and other musicians to join them for a drink. Very rarely does he initiate the drinking experience.
>
> The companion escorts Bud with his approval, to actually prevent anyone from accosting him. In a recent appearance, Bud was actually accosted by a young woman who offered him narcotics. He is not a user and had this woman not been stopped, the situation could have been extremely serious. Bud's companion has been told that he will be given a cash bonus should he assist in any way in the arrest of a person who tries to give Bud any narcotics.

The piece ends by suggesting that Bud needed to play not only to make a living, but for its rehabilitational effect. Throughout 1957, Bud continued to make a living of sorts. He made a second album for Victor, and renewed his recording association with Blue Note, for whom he eventually made three further albums during 1957 and 1958.

New York clubs were not the best environment for Powell, and reports such as Dan Morgenstern's in *Jazz Journal* of August 1958 about his attempts to sit in during Lester Young's 'Thirty Years in Showbusiness' party at Birdland confirm that Bud was too erratic to be sure of being hired. With his 'brown suit, red shirt and blotchy beard', Powell showed signs of considerable physical degeneration. What was needed was a major change, and Bud and Buttercup turned towards France, where, during the 'Birdland' tour, they had encountered many US expatriate musicians making a decent living without the pressures of New York.

Bud Powell playing an unaccompanied set – Paris, the mid-'50s.

CHAPTER 5

FRANCE

Following Bud's visit to Europe with the 'Birdland' package in the autumn of 1956, he did not travel far from New York for some time. However, almost exactly a year after his appearance at the Salle Pleyel, he returned to Paris to play what was intended to be a three-week engagement at the Club Saint-Germain. He opened there on 1 November 1957, and was accompanied by two men who were later to make up his regular trio – Pierre Michelot on bass and Kenny Clarke on drums.

The trip was a consequence of a visit to New York by the French entrepreneur Marcel Romano, who, having heard Powell's 'Birdland' tour concerts, was prepared to offer him an immediate contract to play in Paris for three weeks. As it turned out, the silent, attentive, non-dancing and (relatively speaking) non-drinking audience might have been ideal for Powell, but was certainly not ideal for the club management, who cut short the engagement by a week.

We are fortunate, though, that Powell's enthusiastic champion and supporter Francis Paudras, at the finish of his national service, was on hand to attend these sessions, and he later wrote about them at length in *La Danse des Infidèles*. Most interesting of all his observations is his account of Powell's laboured breathing. In addition to grunting and moaning in unison with his improvisations, Powell would appear to hold his breath during each long right-hand run almost to the point of asphyxiation, rolling his eyes and swaying before catching his breath and plunging on into the next phrase.

Marcel Romano was stuck for engagements for Bud to fill out the last week, so he contacted a band which played on Saturday and Sunday lunchtimes at the Club Saint-Germain. Would their rhythm section, he had asked, be willing to travel out to Fontainebleau, to play for a special concert with Bud Powell and J.

The trio which opened at Club Saint-Germain on 1 November 1957: Kenny Clarke (drums), Powell and Pierre Michelot (bass).

Overleaf p.66

A scene characteristic of the welcome given to American musicians in post-war France. Here, the fêted guest is Coleman Hawkins. Others (left to right) include: Bernard Peiffer, Hubert Fol, Kenny Clarke, (unknown), Pierre Michelot. Both Michelot and Clarke accompanied Powell when he arrived in Paris in November 1957.

J. Johnson? (Ironically, it was to be Johnson's band which was eventually booked to take Powell's place at the Club Saint-Germain.) The drummer, Al Levitt, another American émigré, has written an amusing account of their experiences, which appeared in *Jazz Magazine* as 'Les Silences de Bud'. The band assembled in front of the club in the rue Saint-Benoit. 'We were going to make the journey in an American shooting brake (a Chrysler, I think). It was a very spacious car with plenty of room for everyone and everything. We greeted everyone as they arrived. J.J. was very familiar and friendly, but Bud didn't say a word and shot furious glances at us all.'

During the journey, as the musicians laughed and joked, Bud continued to stare silently and furiously out of the window. His behaviour continued once they had arrived, and J.J., together with Levitt, bassist Paul Rovère and the band's regular pianist René Urtreger, attempted to work out a programme. For the first set, the Frenchmen played as a trio and were then joined by J.J. 'He thanked us, and congratulated the rhythm section. It had really been a pleasure to play with him – he was a master of his instrument and had magnificent timing and feeling.'

During the interval, as the musicians piled into refreshments, Rovère and Levitt, who were to play the next set with Powell, became increasingly uneasy, as Bud sat in a chair, staring fixedly and speaking to nobody. Suddenly the MC announced Bud's name – the public applauded and Bud made hurriedly for the stage. 'We had never expected this, and remained almost literally glued to the spot. Bud . . . realised there was no one behind him. He retraced his steps, and said to Paul and me (with an expression of terror and insecurity on his face), "Tell me, you fellows, aren't you going to play with me?" Paul and I were bowled over, Bud was more nervous than we were . . .'

In the event, all went well, with Bud playing some stupendous trio pieces, and 'behind the soloists he played some of the most stimulating accompaniment one could hope for.' Yet, Levitt remembered, the end of the concert coincided with Bud's return to his silent and staring persona, not even removing his hands from his pockets to shake hands with his fans. The last set had been rounded off with the addition of the young French tenor saxophonist Barney Wilen, who, even though only just twenty, had formed an impressively mature bop style (partly, perhaps, because of an upbringing in the United States which brought him into contact with many leading bop musicians, including the drummer Roy Haynes). Paudras recalls Wilen's contributions to the Club Saint-Germain evenings as some of the most stimulating music played during Powell's visit.

By the end of the year, Powell had gone back to the United States. Occasional press notices show that he continued to appear from time to time in New York, at Birdland and elsewhere, as well as making two further albums for Blue Note. It was announced eventually that he would return to Paris in March 1959, after a fourteen-month absence, to open at the Blue Note Café. This was to be the trip during which Powell decided to stay on in Paris; he remained there until the late summer of 1964.

Before coming to France, Bud had once more been unwell, and he was released from King's County Hospital in Brooklyn not long before his departure. Buttercup told Robert Perlongo: 'Nobody gave him much longer to live. Not even me for a while there. His liver, you know, was very bad. He had to keep taking these Vitamin B-12 tablets all the time.'

Powell's drinking continued, and was the major problem. His fellow musicians were aware of the dangers of giving him alcohol, and tried to keep him from it, kidding him about it. They also called him 'the old man', but in some senses this was a mark of respect for an old master aged thirty-six. An apocryphal story tells of Powell going into a Paris bar on his first trip. He reached the bar as one of the regulars fell comatose from his stool. Powell watched in admiration: 'I'll have one of those', he said.

Jackie McLean recalled: 'One little glass of brandy can completely flip him around – I've never seen juice affect anybody like that.'

Another effect of the alcohol was evident in Powell's physical appearance. He had put on weight, and his swollen hands and neck gave him an almost oriental appearance. Francis Paudras observed that this was coupled with a propensity to wear collars that were a bit too tight, so that Bud always presented a slightly uncomfortable looking figure when dressed in the formal suit and tie required for his club appearances.

Bud opened at the Blue Note in March 1959 with Pierre Michelot and Kenny Clarke. Even so fervent an admirer as Paudras admitted that the music was uneven, but that particularly in the first few evenings Bud regained some of his prodigious talents. The trio was to become known as 'Les Trois Patrons' (the three bosses), and obtained a remarkable degree of unity. Clarke, in particular, was able to follow Powell 'like his shadow', and, of all the bassists with whom Clarke was to work in Europe, he singled out Michelot as his favourite. Interviewed by Jean-Louis Ginibre for *Jazz Magazine* (March 1985), Clarke said: 'Michelot is the sole bassist in whose work I take real pleasure, of all those I've played with in Europe . . . People talk a lot about Niels-Henning Ørsted Pedersen, but even today I prefer Michelot.'

DINNERS   DANCING

27, Rue d'Artois
BAL zac 18-92   PARIS-VIIIe

For Michelot himself, it was an unusual experience. He told Paudras: 'Contact with Bud was difficult. He didn't say anything, and my English was far from good . . . but there were no problems over the music. It was simple. When it was time to play, Bud sat at the piano and began. It was up to me to follow what he was playing.'

After the residency at the Blue Note, Powell played odd gigs at the Caméléon, and then in July opened at Le Chat Qui Pêche in a trio with bassist Chuck Israels (who had been studying in Paris) and drummer J. T. Hogan. Paudras recalls the club as very hot, humid and smoky and the music as a barrage of breakneck hard bop, with Hogan's loud drums reminiscent of Elvin Jones's unremitting style. The trio played few ballads.

It was during this residency that the friendship between Powell and Paudras began. Paudras was a commercial artist and draughtsman, who had studied the piano seriously and had collected Powell's records avidly. Attending Bud's regular sessions at the Blue Note had left him barely able to afford to live, let alone attend Le Chat Qui Pêche. Listening from the street outside through the ventilators of the subterranean club, Paudras heard much of the music, and encountered Bud as the pianist left to spend his intervals in the bar opposite, the Storyville, run by the father of the saxophonist Maxim Saury. Bud would try and sponge a drink off any likely prospect, and Paudras not only bought him glasses of beer, but struck up a conversation of sorts – mainly on account of Bud's incredulity at hearing himself on the jukebox. This gained Francis free admission to Bud's sessions at Le Chat, and their friendship grew from there.

Following the engagement at Le Chat, Bud was asked to play in various parts of Europe, but his home base continued to be Paris. He lived in the Saint-Germain area in the Hôtel Louisiane. A number of other musicians lived there, and to some extent the hotel was the base for the expatriate Americans who had made Paris their home. The drummer Kansas Fields was a regular tenant, and he and Buttercup presided over communal meals. The air would be heavy with the scent of Gauloises and soul food. To outside eyes, this was an ideal, protective environment for Powell. In reality, he became increasingly withdrawn, and suffered considerable indignities at the hands of Buttercup, who collected his earnings and held his passport and papers, effectively denying him any degree of independence. As the months passed, regular observers noticed an air of almost canine subservience appear in Powell.

In one respect, Bud retained his independence. His habit was to take a constitutional through the quarter where he lived, and

Drummer Kansas Fields, resident at the Hôtel Louisiane, seen here with pianist Mary Lou Williams and bassist Buddy Banks.

Francis Paudras was amazed to see Powell walking several feet ahead of Buttercup and her young son, apparently ignoring them completely. At the first sign of a familiar face, Powell asked for a 'ballon de vin rouge', and escaped with Paudras to the terrace of a nearby café, leaving Buttercup to wend her way. This became a regular custom, and Paudras began to keep an eye open for Powell as he walked along the rue de Seine.

In the final months of the year, Bud returned to the Blue Note. He worked with Jimmy Gourlay and Lucky Thompson. His trio, with Michelot and Clarke, together with Barney Wilen, made some recordings on 12 December that were later to be issued as part of a compilation of Americans in Paris. On 18 December, Bud accompanied Francis Paudras to a concert at the Théâtre des Champs-Elysées given by Art Blakey's Jazz Messengers. Paudras had invited Powell in all innocence, thinking he would enjoy the concert. To his great consternation, Blakey announced Bud from the stage, calling him up to play with the band. The results were recorded and later issued. It was only afterwards that Paudras discovered that Bud's guest appearance had been announced in the jazz press, and that Bud (in a manner later to manifest itself in many deadpan jokes) had played along with Francis's innocent invitation as if unaware of the concert.

Early in 1960, Paudras moved to a studio apartment at 65 rue Boursault, which was to play a decisive role in the story of Powell. When the Blue Note engagement came to an end, Powell stopped playing in public, and seemed to fade from the scene. Jean Wagner, in an early account of Paudras's involvement with Powell for *Jazz Magazine*, wrote: 'He didn't have any more work. Again and again, stories appeared in the jazz press, foretelling the eclipse of this particular star. Friends, full of good intentions, told Francis

The daily constitutional: Buttercup, her son, and Bud.

Paudras that Bud wandered the streets aimlessly, completely out of work. He was badly dressed, pitiable, like a down and out.'

Paudras decided to contact Bud directly. He told Wagner: 'There wasn't a single reason why Bud shouldn't come to [my] house, and, who knows, become [my] friend.'

Wagner continued the story: 'When Francis arrived at the hotel in the rue de Seine, Bud was shut in his room. A bare desolate room, like that of a monk. He was in his vest. Bud appeared to understand only one thing from all that Francis said to him and his entourage: he was going to get out. He could be free for a few hours. A few minutes later, he was on his way to the rue Boursault where Francis had his rooms. The adventure began.'

As early as this first visit, Paudras stumbled across the principal reason for the erratic nature of Powell's performances. As they left the Louisiane, Paudras was handed a couple of sachets, with the advice to ensure that Bud took them within sixteen hours. 'Bud is extremely nervous, they are necessary to keep him calm.' The drug turned out to be Largactyl, a treatment available for the treatment of schizophrenics only under strict medical supervision. Its principal characteristic was to induce sleep, yet in Powell's case it appeared merely to subdue him. It quickly became obvious to Paudras, as Powell became a regular visitor to his flat, and as he observed Powell during a short rebooking at the Blue Note, that Bud was constantly fighting a lethargy induced by this treatment. That he managed to play at all was remarkable, given that he sometimes went on stage after taking the drug. It is hardly surprising, since Buttercup apparently gradually increased the doses, that critics noticed that Bud was often unable to attain his customary speed at the keyboard, and that some of his glittering runs petered out in mid-phrase. How Buttercup continued to obtain the Largactyl is unclear, but she used it to keep the man she referred to as her 'breadwinner' in a docile condition in which she found it easy to control him. It is also likely that the immediate and catastrophic effect of alcohol on Powell's system was in no small way due to its reaction with this drug. He continued to take Largactyl until the end of 1962, when he effectively moved in with Paudras and his wife-to-be, Nicole, and the medicament was stopped once and for all.

As early as January 1960, Paudras established a good enough rapport with Powell for the pianist to confide in him that Buttercup was not his real wife. Kenny Clarke confirmed this, adding (in support of Goodstein's earlier testimony) that Powell could not have been Johnny's father. Nevertheless, Paudras did not interfere at this stage with Buttercup's control of Bud's affairs. She continued to book his tours, club appearances and record dates.

Perhaps rallied by his friendship with Paudras, Bud began to work again. In February 1960, under the auspices of the RTF, he toured France with Oscar Pettiford and Kenny Clarke, and this was followed in April by a trip to Essen with the same trio, which recorded with Coleman Hawkins.

In June 1960, Bud was recorded with Clarke and Michelot. A month later, he sat in with Mingus and Dannie Richmond for a long performance of *I'll Remember April* at the Antibes Festival. Powell had professed little admiration for Eric Dolphy, and it is significant that, when Dolphy and Booker Ervin joined the rhythm section to trade fours on the final choruses, Powell left the stage and did not return.

On 8 September, Oscar Pettiford died in Copenhagen. With his death, Bud lost the third member of what had briefly been a very successful trio. He played for Pettiford's memorial in Paris at the Blue Note. With Clarke and Michelot he recorded a tribute album at a concert in memory of Pettiford, held at the Théâtre des Champs-Elysées on 14 October.

During the autumn of 1960 and the early part of 1961, the rhythm of Bud's life became settled. He continued to live at the Louisiane, under Buttercup's domination, and she continued to treat him with Largactyl. From time to time he would be confined to his room by the simple expedient of Buttercup taking away his trousers. His afternoons would frequently be spent at Paudras's apartment, where the young artist worked at his commercial designs while Bud sat about and occasionally played the piano. Bud would affect to read the newspaper, but had in reality acquired little or no French. He could ask fluently for 'un ballon de vin rouge', but this tested his grasp of the language to its limits. Lost in a world of his own, and caught up in the inertia of mind and body produced by his treatment with Largactyl, he was at least once caught holding the paper upside down.

Paudras recalls, in *La Danse des Infidèles*, that about this time he was involved in promotional designs for a smart new cocktail. The manufacturers thought it would be chic to identify the drink

Mingus and Bud reunited – with Buttercup.

with jazz, and Francis engaged Ellington and Armstrong (who were in France to work on Martin Ritt's film *Paris Blues*) to attend the launch. This was the beginning of a friendship with Duke which led indirectly to a Powell recording session in early 1963, supervised by Ellington.

Press reports of Powell's playing in early 1961 suggest that it was erratic. Nevertheless, at the end of April Bud left for a tour of Italy with a trio comprising the bassist Jacques Hess and his drummer from the 1950s in the USA, Art Taylor. They played a series of concerts opposite Thelonious Monk. Hess recounted to Paudras the events of one concert during which Bud appeared to fall asleep in mid-tune. When Hess looked across, Powell was staring absently at his watch. He came alive at Hess's urgent shouts to wake up, and picked up the exact place in the piece in mid-bar. Events such as this occurred with increasing frequency as the effects of the Largactyl made themselves evident.

During the latter part of 1961, when Bud did work, it was with the Michelot–Clarke trio. They recorded together, including a session where they backed Don Byas. By all accounts Bud's spirits were at a low ebb, and this continued into the early part of 1962. In April of that year, Bud toured Switzerland, Sweden and Denmark. There are unconfirmed rumours of Bud having severe mental health problems in Switzerland. His playing in Stockholm was uninspired, but in Denmark, at the Montmartre Club, he found an enthusiastic audience and sympathetic support from drummer William Schioppfe and the fifteen-year-old bassist Niels-Henning Ørsted Pedersen. He was apparently filmed for Danish Television during this period, and it was almost certainly during this trip that he made the short film *Stopforbud*, showing him in Copenhagen relaxing and at work. The film has a commentary by Dexter Gordon, who became a Copenhagen resident himself later in 1962.

In the early autumn of 1962, Bud took the opportunity offered by his regular job at the Blue Note to run away from Buttercup and her regime. Instead of coming back after his accustomed departure from the club during the interval to scrounge a glass of wine or beer off a willing fan, he simply walked out into the night. (At this stage, even beer had so dramatic an effect on him that great efforts were made by the club management to prevent Bud drinking.)

Paudras found him in a general ward at the Hospital Laënnec. It was, he told Jean Wagner, 'A large dirty common ward, with cracked and peeling walls. And in the beds, indifferent, resigned men.' For some days Powell was confused and silent, although a visit from Paudras and friends with a meal of oysters and other *fruits de mer* produced a momentary rally. An orderly told Paudras: 'He's an impossible patient. He refuses to comply with

Bud's 'accustomed departure . . . during the interval to scrounge a glass of wine or beer off a willing fan'. The fan here is English journalist Mike Hennessey.

the hospital regime, and will not allow us to conduct the necessary medical examinations.' This sounded warning bells in Paudras's mind, but, unfortunately, too late. When he returned the next day, Powell was gone.

'The room was still full, but Bud wasn't there.

'"Where is Bud?"

'"We made enquiries at the American Embassy. We found out that before coming to France, Mr Powell had been a patient in a psychiatric ward. Since his attitude here was far from normal, he's gone to a psychiatric cell."'

What followed, during the next twenty-four hours, can only be described as a Kafkaesque search through the bureaucracy of the hospital system. Starting his enquiries at nine in the morning, Paudras found no trace of Bud for six hours. When he eventually tracked him down, another series of arguments followed over whether Paudras (as a non-relation) might be able to see him. Eventually allowed access to Powell's cell, Bud pleaded with him: 'Francis, get me out of here. Please, I beg you.'

In a curious way, history repeated itself. Just as Elmo Hope had discovered a young doctor sympathetic to Bud's case who was able to help Powell out of Creedmore, so Paudras found a kindred spirit in the young man who came to examine Powell in his Parisian ward. Paudras listened in on a long and sympathetic interview with Bud, at which Powell admitted to dreaming at night that he was constantly playing the piano, and that, even when awake, he was prone to the same dreams. In these he battled against fatigue at the keyboard (just as he obviously did in reality). He talked of the horrors of his electric shock treatment in the United States and how this had not only destroyed his sexual abilities, but played havoc with his creative powers.

At long last, the young doctor signed Bud out of the care of the

Bud Powell.

hospital and into that of Paudras. Although, at first, Powell was billetted at a hotel near Paudras's flat, he effectively moved in with Francis and Nicole. Bud's nocturnal habits of playing the piano did not endear him to the neighbours. Petitions were signed, protests were made. Somehow or another, Paudras mollified his fellow tenants, and for the last weeks of 1962 and most of the early months of 1963 the menage continued at the rue Boursault. Powell took a long time to rehabilitate himself. He stopped taking Largactyl, and he was limited in his intake of red wine. He began to take an interest in life again, and eventually asked to be taken to the Cigale (a club which featured the expatriate US jazzmen Benny Waters and Jack Butler).

In his autobiography, Benny Waters described this as 'a cafe providing entertainment, situated in Pigalle, the red district of Paris'. Benny played there on and off for ten years, from 1954 to 1964, and briefly again in the late 1960s. Seeing Powell come into the club on his first public sortie after his hospital stay, Benny (an incurable extrovert) announced the visitor, and asked if he'd care to play something with the band. Bud grabbed Francis's arm, and ran out of the club as quickly as possible.

The following night, however, Bud asked to return. Unbidden, he slipped into the pianist's chair and launched into fifty choruses of *Get Happy* at a furious tempo. Paudras recalls the signs of fatigue amongst the other musicians, and the relentless energy that Powell put into his playing, as if in a trance. Waters eventually brought the number to a close by playing the theme under Bud's solo lines until the whole band finished together on the tune. His point made, Bud left the stage and walked out of the club. A turning point had been reached, and he was ready to perform again in public, on his own terms.

This incident is central to the extraordinary account of Powell and Paudras's friendship in *La Danse des Infidèles*. As a piece of autobiographical writing it is a remarkably honest picture of a man obsessed. Paudras willingly admits his preoccupation with Powell was such that it ruled many aspects of his life. For instance, during one of Powell's tours away from Paris, Paudras planned a holiday in Spain. The car piled high with luggage, he was about to set off when the postman delivered a new Bud Powell record, sent by a specialist mail-order shop. So keen was Paudras to hear it that he unpacked the car and postponed his departure by three days, in order to feel that he had listened adequately to the disc before leaving for a holiday with no record player.

The Cigale event marks the moment when, for the duration of Bud's remaining period in Paris, he began to emerge from Buttercup's control and started to appear in public with all the

Powell during his Paris renaissance.

advantages of his new domicile with Paudras. Gradually, Paudras helped Bud to establish his confidence and dignity again, even if Buttercup still diverted Bud's earnings into her own pocket and held on to his papers. She also made no efforts to release his suitcases after they were held at an airport during one of Bud's tours, and for several weeks, until Paudras located his wardrobe, Powell wore the same clothes all the time. In due course, Paudras bought a new apartment in which Bud had his own room, and he made slow progress to wean Bud from his addiction to alcohol. The high points of Powell's playing in 1963 show a man no longer fighting lethargy and thoughtless indignities. On his May session with Dexter Gordon he displays an awareness of his limitations, and considerable control.

With the arrival of Johnny Griffin in Paris in 1963, Bud (who had been refused his old job back at the Blue Note) sat in with his band. Just as he had done at the Cigale, he managed a flow of energy that proved he had recaptured some of his old control, and he was reinstated at the club. He remained there for some months, with bassist Gilbert Rovère and drummer Larry Ritchie, playing alternate sets with his fellow expatriate Kenny Drew. Sets at the club (which was at 27 rue d'Artois) began nightly at eight, and there was a Sunday 'tea dance' from 15.30 to 19.30.

In late February, Powell recorded for Reprise with Rovère and Kansas Fields. This was the session supervised by Ellington, who had set it up through Paudras after hearing of Bud's recovery and new-found energy. There were some fears that Fields would not get on well with Bud at the session, since he was a resident of the Louisiane with Buttercup, and she had nominated him for the date. She also took control of the finances, but Bud had asked that she stay away from the actual recording, and she did so. She was co-operative on this occasion, but the same helpful spirit did not extend to a project to make a film called *The Amazing Bud Powell*, initiated by the Jamaican writer Lebert Bethure. The *Melody Maker* announced on 13 June 1963: 'Bud Powell Film Ready'. It went on to say that Bud was seen 'playing and living in Paris. Shooting began in June, and the film is now in the editing stage.' According to Paudras, Buttercup prevented this from being finished, owing to her contractual demands.

Paudras recounts that the broadcaster Henri Renaud interviewed Powell for the radio at about this time. The transcript given in *La Danse des Infidèles* accords exactly with the text,

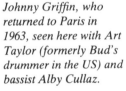

Johnny Griffin, who returned to Paris in 1963, seen here with Art Taylor (formerly Bud's drummer in the US) and bassist Alby Cullaz.

wrongly ascribed to 15 January 1963 on Elektra Musician E1-60030. The voice of Powell is intercut, on that recording, with that of a French announcer (possibly Renaud, or possibly Paudras) and several references are made to Powell's illness. It is probable that both short interviews preserved on that disc belong to the following year. This is likely because Powell became seriously ill in early September 1963, and both discussions refer to this illness.

Alarmed by Powell's weight loss and breathlessness (Paudras's new apartment was at the top of five flights of stairs), Francis arranged for Bud to see a doctor. The diagnosis was a complete shock. Powell had advanced tuberculosis, was highly infectious,

A sequence of shots of Powell in Paris, taken at about the time of the abortive film project The Amazing Bud Powell.

and might survive only a short time. Few, if any, of Powell's intimates were actually infected, although Nicole, Paudras's wife-to-be, was mildly unwell, and had to be treated. Powell, on the other hand, betrayed an irrational fear (or, given his background, perhaps an entirely rational fear) of hospitals, and ran away. After a three-day police search, he was eventually run to ground and admitted on 17 September to the Hospital Foch. It turned out that this was not a moment too soon, and he was found to have a seven-centimetre hole in one lung.

At this moment, the remarkable Oscar Goodstein came to Bud's aid. He rallied round and sent money to cover hospital costs,

but his first attempts were intercepted by Buttercup, who still held all Powell's papers and presented herself to the US Embassy as Powell's wife. Paudras reprints much of the acrimonious correspondence which followed.

On 2 November, *Melody Maker* reported that Goodstein had held a benefit for Bud at Birdland, starring Dizzy Gillespie, Thelonious Monk, Stan Getz and Gerry Mulligan, 'all proceeds going to the ailing pianist . . . reportedly suffering from tuberculosis, and confined to bed in the Hospital Foch, Paris.' A cheque for $415.28 was sent, and apparently this time reached Paudras.

On 19 November, Bud transferred from the hospital to the

Bouffemont Sanitorium. He had made remarkable progress, and no longer needed intensive hospital care, but, like so many TB patients, now needed the sustained rest offered by a nursing home or sanitorium. His holed lung had mended sufficiently well to avoid an operation, and the *Melody Maker* was clearly acting on slightly out-of-date news when it ran the story in its 12 December issue: 'Bud Powell, in a Paris hospital with tuberculosis, is so gravely ill that his friends fear the end may be near.'

Powell was allowed home to Paudras's flat for Christmas, and thereafter, for some months, came out regularly at weekends. Paudras suggests that Buttercup had little contact with Bud at this time, although he believes she obtained a power of attorney from him which gave her more clout in trying to intercept any money which was sent to him c/o the US Embassy. It is certain that she visited him at Bouffemont, however, since Lindsay Barrett describes a visit to the sanitorium in the company of Buttercup, her son John, Sonny Rollins and his wife Elinor, and a Richard Anderson. Powell was allowed out, and they went to the local Cafe des Sports, where he drank beer. They were alarmed when he insisted on a cognac and then more beer and a vin rouge – unable to apply any discipline or resist temptation. A similar story surrounds two jazz lovers who took him out for the evening in Paris, taking him inadvisedly to the Blue Note. He ended up in the cold, wet night taking a taxi to Buttercup to beg for money. Barrett's account presents a marginally different aspect of Powell's illness from that of Paudras. The latter tends to emphasise the best sides of Powell's character and behaviour, and stresses Powell's serious attempts to avoid alcohol in Paudras's company.

Francis took Bud to meet Monk as he passed through Paris airport on 23 February 1964. Powell was slowly growing back into normal life, but was financially in desperate straits over the cost of his treatment. On 13 March 1964 a benefit was held for him at the Salle Wagram in Paris.

All through his illness, the Blue Note had continued to advertise the Trois Patrons. When he was finally fit enough to play, Bud returned to the club. He played only the first sets, and, despite the hoarding, his trio included bassist Michel Gaudry and drummer Larry Ritchie (later replaced by Art Taylor). Goodstein offered Powell the chance to pay off some of his debts with a residency at Birdland. The chance to return to New York arrived at an opportune moment in Bud's rehabilitation. He had (at Paudras's insistence) been paid direct by the management of the Blue Note after his return from Bouffemont, cutting Buttercup out of the deal. Goodstein's offer appealed to Powell's new found belief in his ability to manage himself and his finances, and he accepted.

Paudras found himself torn between his awareness that New York would probably do Powell no good at all (and hence a desire to accompany him there), and the news that Nicole was pregnant. The three set off for a friend's boarding house at Edenville, a small seaside resort on the west coast of the Cherbourg peninsula, a few kilometres south of Granville.

Bud played with a local bassist and drummer in a restaurant there, and they were joined for a few days by Johnny Griffin. The summer passed quickly, and after much discussion it was agreed that Francis would go with Bud to New York, even though there was a strong chance Nicole might give birth during his absence. The month or so spent by the sea had restored Bud to health, and he seemed more stable than at any time during his stay in France. It was a risk, but the signs were that Bud would be more able than ever before to cope with the pressures of New York – and, besides, he could always return to the security of his new adopted home in Paris.

CHAPTER 6

LAST DAYS IN NEW YORK

'People think Bud is crazy or lost or silent but he really is in a state of grace.'
Francis Paudras

For some time there had been rumours in New York that Powell would be returning. He and Paudras arrived on 16 August 1964, at Kennedy airport. They were met by Oscar Goodstein, who praised Paudras: 'Without this man, Bud might not be with us today.' The news report in *Down Beat* gave due credit to Paudras for nursing Powell back to health and shielding him from undesirable influences.

Powell was asked what he was most looking forward to now that he was back in the United States. His reply was revealing. 'Handling my own dough', he said. This was his way of saying that he was no longer willing to be supervised.

He had a long engagement at Birdland, where he was received on the opening night with a standing ovation before he played a note. That night he reached great heights of inspiration in his own *John's Abbey*, and Monk's *Bemsha Swing* and *Epistrophy*. He stayed at Birdland until the end of September, except for one week when he recorded an album for Roulette. The album shows his playing to be erratic and inconsistent, reflecting reports of his work at the club. There were, however, contradictory reports which suggested he was wonderful. Still others said he was poor, and commented that he sounded sad.

On 10 October Powell did not show up at the club. He was missing for two days and was then found at the house of friends in Brooklyn. With this alarming sign that he was slipping into the old, bad habits, it was decided that Powell and Paudras should return to Paris. Then Powell disappeared again on 18 October.

He was seen at a party given by Baroness Nica de Koenigswarter, at her home in Weehawken, New Jersey, in October. The Baroness had long been a patroness of jazz. She was a member of the English branch of the international Rothschild family. Her husband was the Baron Jules de Koenigswarter, an official of the French diplomatic corps. In Mexico in 1951, she tired of the life of a diplomat's wife and came alone to New York to pursue her interest in jazz, and took a luxuriously furnished apartment in the Hotel Stanhope on Fifth Avenue.

She was hostess to musicians, providing drinks and dinners. Her apartment has been described as an 'elegant crash pad'. Musicians came and went at all hours. Records were played all the time and there was even the occasional jam session, said to have been subdued in deference to other residents. However, these other residents were disturbed by it all and the Baroness avoided eviction by using her title and influence and the force of her personality. Her rent, however, was doubled. She became known as the jazz baroness and was celebrated in several jazz numbers: Monk's *Pannonica*, Freddie Redd's *Nica Steps Out*, and Gigi Gryce's *Nica's Tempo*. It was Monk who first brought Parker to her apartment and it was to her apartment that Parker went to die in 1955.

Powell slipped out of the Baroness's party while the others were talking. He did not return until 23 October. He was seen in a doorway the day before in Greenwich Village by the photographer, later record producer, Don Schlitten, who was on his way to the Village Vanguard club. Schlitten tried to persuade Powell to come with him, at least to phone Goodstein. Powell was only interested in begging a drink. Unsuccessful, he walked away.

Powell returned to the Baroness's home. He was in good spirits and, according to attorney Bernard Stollman, 'talking more volubly than usual'. Powell and Paudras were due to leave New York for Paris on 27 October. It was assumed they had left together but people were later surprised to learn that Paudras had gone on alone and that Powell, with no plans to return to France, was living with friends in Brooklyn.

In March 1965, Powell appeared at a memorial concert at Carnegie Hall to celebrate the tenth anniversary of Charlie Parker's death. There was no inconsistency in the reports about his playing that night. The best said it was laborious, the worst were embarrassed by his performance. He had put on more weight by this time and appeared bloated. His eyes were vacant as he shuffled to the piano. He played the Horace Silver composition *No Smoking*. This was usually taken at a brisk tempo. Gitler, in *Jazz Masters*, said it 'sounded like a 78 rpm record being played at 45'; and '*Round Midnight*, although negotiated at a pace closer to what Powell seemed capable of on that evening, was almost equally disturbing. It was indeed difficult to look at or listen to Bud that night.'

The attorney Bernard Stollman became his manager. Powell worked only occasionally. He was presented on a bill with what were described as 'New Thing' avant-garde players, Albert Ayler and Milford Graves. Powell was considered to be in better form than at the disappointing and distressing Carnegie Hall appearance. Critic Dan Morgenstern wrote: 'Powell was far from his peak. However, his final selection, *I Remember Clifford*, was extremely moving and what had seemed to be faltering time on the faster pieces now became a nearly Monkish deliberateness, each phrase ringing out full and strong. What Powell hasn't lost is his marvellous touch and sound, and everything he played revealed a

A late shot of Powell during his last year in New York.

92

sense of balance and proportion not much in evidence elsewhere on the program.'

He had lost his health for good now. He lived in Brooklyn and worked only sporadically. His liver was giving serious trouble and he went into hospital, but recovered briefly after several critical days.

Those who had said 'Bud's come home to die' were proved right: he died on the night of August 1/2 in King's County Hospital, Brooklyn. The death certificate put causes of death as tuberculosis, malnutrition and alcoholism. 'I further certify', wrote Dr H. Eisenberg on Powell's death certificate (issued at King's County Hospital), 'that death was not caused directly or indirectly by accident, homicide, suicide, acute or chronic poisoning, or any suspicious or unusual manner, and that it was due to natural causes.'

Perhaps 'natural causes' was the right phrase to use. Life itself was the main cause. Pure medical facts could not admit to that, nor that Powell had been driven onwards and then down by the demon in him that also made him create some of the finest jazz piano ever heard.

Marc Crawford said he knew he was dying slowly but did not care. 'He wanted to be where they were', Buttercup said, referring to musical colleagues who were dead. She thought he had that in mind when he said his last words: 'I'll be alright.' She thought he meant he was going to be with them.

Later words from the drummer Elvin Jones sympathetically summed up Powell's life and career: 'I always had the impression that Bud had been hurt so much. He was like a very delicate piece of china. I think he was an extremely sensitive person, a very beautiful person. He was really nice and I loved him. I thought he was a genius in what he was doing. His ideas about modern music were revolutionary. There are very few pianists even now who have approached the level of proficiency which Bud Powell attained and consistently maintained. He's one of the masters.'

Pianist Hampton Hawes, who was heavily influenced by Powell, was more succinct: 'Bud Powell was the greatest be-bop piano player in the world. Nobody could phrase like him. I met Bud, but I didn't get to know him well.'

The funeral involved a huge procession through Harlem. The coffin was preceded by the 'Jazzmobile'. On it pianist Barry Harris and trumpeter Lee Morgan played 'Round Midnight, Dance Of The Infidels and Bud's Bubble. An estimated 5000 people lined the streets to say goodbye.

CHAPTER 7

THE RECORDINGS

This chapter provides a commentary on the recordings outlined in the chronology that follows. The issues and reissues of material are too complex for a brief survey to comprehend, so wherever possible tracks are identified by their original issue. Dates are as in the chronology.

The first recordings by Powell are those with Cootie Williams. On the small-group recordings from January 1944, Powell has several chorus-length solos. His playing on the ballads *My Old Flame* and *Sweet Lorraine* echoes that of Art Tatum. There are passages with strong bop inflections on *Honeysuckle Rose* and behind Williams's vocal on *Gotta Do Some War Work Baby*. Although the band's style is transitional, part swing, part bop, Powell's solo on *Floogie Boo* is completely in the new idiom, as is his playing on *I Don't Know*, where he goes into the double time that was to be one of his trademarks. As examples of music in transition, this is an interesting set – Powell's work contrasts vividly with that of the established soloists Eddie 'Lockjaw' Davis, Eddie 'Cleanhead' Vinson and Williams himself.

The big band's material and style were sufficiently rooted in swing to offer fewer opportunities to hear Powell's conception of bop piano, though he is heard on *Blue Garden Blues*. The stay with Williams was the longest sustained engagement of Powell's career. Temperamentally, even in the early years, he liked to lead groups and to take control of his material. Sometimes, this determination turned into wilful obstinacy and caused problems. On one occasion with Williams, Cootie apparently called a number and Powell announced he did not want to play it. Allan Morrison, in *Ebony*, wrote: 'Cootie, by this time used to the pianist's peculiarities, pursed his lips impatiently and repeated the title of the tune. Bud folded his arms over the keyboard and stared at the ceiling. "I won't play it," he told Cootie. Cootie finally compromised on another tune.'

Kenny Clarke – leader of the 5 September 1946 session.

After leaving Williams, Powell appeared on numerous recording dates in 1946 and 1947, usually with what were more or less regular working groups. He is pianist on four tracks (plus three alternate takes) with a quintet led by tenorist Dexter Gordon in January 1946. The inferior trumpet of Leonard Haskins completes the front line, contrasting with the thick-toned maturing tenor of Gordon. Drummer Max Roach and bassist Curly Russell make up the quintet. Powell solos on *Dexter Digs In* and *Long Tall Dexter*. Just as he had when accompanying Pearl Bailey, the singer with Cootie Williams, Powell again proved himself a sympathetic accompanist behind Sarah Vaughan on a record date arranged by Tadd Dameron in May 1946. Powell is one of a sextet, including Kenny Clarke on drums, Leo Parker on baritone saxophone and Freddy Webster on trumpet, alongside nine strings.

Powell appeared with Jay Jay Johnson's Be-boppers, the group led by the rapid-fire be-bop trombonist J. J. Johnson, on four tracks from 26 June 1946 – *Coppin' The Bop, Jay Jay, Mad Be Bop* and *Jay Bird*. To modern listeners these tracks have a dated air, set alight only by Powell and Johnson.

In September, with a nine-piece group led by Kenny Clarke, which included Fats Navarro and Kenny Dorham on trumpets and Sonny Stitt on alto, Powell recorded four titles. Two of the four are by Thelonious Monk: *Epistrophy* and *52nd St Theme*. The others are *Oop Bop Sh-bam* and *Rue Chaptal*. All the musicians are featured at some reasonable length on one or more of the sides. Powell was now beginning to sound startling. Here, his drive, his precise timing and the definition of his phrasing are effective and affecting.

The next day he was part of an all-star group, the Be-Bop Boys, again with Clarke, Stitt, Dorham and Navarro. Two takes each were made of *Fat Boy, Webb City, Boppin' A Riff*, and *Everything's Cool*, and on them Powell contributes long, intense solos. *Webb City* is a Powell original and almost the first definitive example of his mature style. Pianist Freddie Redd said of it: 'That's Bud Powell!'

In January 1947 Powell recorded eight trio performances for the Deluxe label: *Somebody Loves Me, Bud's Bubble, I Should Care, I'll Remember April, Indiana, Nice Work If You Can Get It, Everything Happens To Me* and Monk's *Off Minor*. The trio was completed by bassist Curly Russell and drummer Max Roach. This trio was working regularly on 52nd Street at the time. Unfortunately, the Deluxe company went out of business soon afterwards and the tracks were not issued until Roost records brought them out in 1949.

The recordings consist of eight masterpieces of jazz piano and must have appeared as a revelation at the time. Here is Powell at his peak, setting the standards his imitators failed to meet. Russell and Roach give Powell some of the best support he ever found. Of the drummers of the time Max Roach and Roy Haynes were the two who worked best with the pianist. Later in his career he was to suffer from unsympathetic drummers, but, playing up to ninety bars a minute, Powell was always difficult for drummers. Great control of the brushes is required to give a firm but light push to such a pianist.

On these 1947 recordings, Powell was fit and composed, his concentration was total, his touch and timing were exact, and the notes flowed in a precise torrent, each standing out clear and sharp. Every track proves why Powell remained without rival in the late 1940s and early 1950s. Mary Lou Williams described his technique to Max Jones: 'He is the only pianist who makes every note ring. The strength in his fingers must be unequalled.'

His control of what for others would be reckless speed is shown on *Indiana*, which rockets along at eighty-eight bars to the minute, and *Bud's Bubble*, at seventy-four bars. Both are breath-taking for their invention and cohesion. *Bud's Bubble* bursts into a flood of rhythmic complexity and switched accents, with a strongly effective left hand which prompts first quietly and then violently. His approach to the medium-tempo pieces such as *Somebody Loves Me* is as complex. The ballads *I Should Care* and *Everything Happens To Me* are examples of what came to be atypical of Powell's contemplative playing – strong, pared-down, hard-centred examinations of the romantic. Here, too, is *Off Minor*, an early sign of his commitment to Monk.

A direct comparison of this playing with that from the session of September 1953 (with George Duvivier on bass and Art Taylor on drums) points to the changes that were to come. The titles from this date – which include *My Heart Stood Still, You'd Be So Nice To Come Home To, Burt Covers Bud* and *Embraceable You* – show how, in six years, Bud's timing was beginning to be suspect, his lines starting to become less lengthy and somewhat fragmentary. His invention is not sustained. The mood is almost bleak and the touch is not as precise or clear. *Embraceable You* is the outstanding track. Heavy chords are now a device for emotional effect. With his technique declining, Powell's chord playing had to become an essential device now that his long, single-note lines could not be so well realised. The directness of *Embraceable You* is disturbing. Behind this, and the other tracks of the session, there is still an exceptional talent at work.

On 4 May 1947, Powell made his one and only studio recording date with Charlie Parker. (Some early accounts suggested he was on the 26 November 1945 date when Parker recorded *Ko-Ko*, but it is clear that the pianist on that occasion was Argonne Thornton [Sadik Hakim].) Several takes of four titles – *Donna Lee, Chasing The Bird, Buzzy* and *Cheryl* – were recorded by a quintet which also included Miles Davis, Tommy Potter on bass and Max Roach. There is an apparent tension in the session, which is attributed by many critics to friction between Powell and Parker. What is certainly the case is that when, shortly after the recording session, this quintet began a residency at the Three Deuces, Powell had been replaced by Duke Jordan.

The tracks were recorded for Savoy. As can be seen from the chronology, they were released in dribs and drabs, but the entire recording date forms part of the 'Complete Savoy Studio Sessions' under Parker's name. This is a five-album set (Savoy S5J 5500) that comprehends all takes, including the rejected takes and false starts. Parker recorded for Savoy from 1944 to 1948 and the whole set is an essential document of bop. It is also a fascinating record of Parker's development over the period and, more important, an insight into Parker's method of making recordings: his approach to reworking a tune, subsequent takes varying immensely until he was satisfied.

Sixteen cuts fully document the four titles that include Powell. The session was held in New York just after Parker had returned from California after his breakdown, having been away from New York for eighteen months. The rhythm section had been working 52nd Street as the Bud Powell Trio. Powell dominates the date. Parker and Davis are below their best; both fluff runs and miss notes, and Parker appears to be bothered by reed trouble. Powell is masterly whether giving relaxed, spare, but pushing chording behind the soloists or offering what are amongst his finest blues solos on *Buzzy* and *Cheryl*.

Powell was recorded on several other occasions with Parker, but these were all unofficial live recordings, made in clubs, from the radio, or, in the case of the Massey Hall concert, by one of the musicians. Amongst the best of the live recordings is one made by Fats Navarro, Parker and Powell, backed by Curly Russell and Art Blakey. Fragments of this session have been widely issued on a variety of labels, but the bulk is on a double-album set 'One Night at Birdland' (CBS 88250). Some issues have implied that this material was recorded at various times, possibly at Café Society on 8 or 15 May 1950. But most authorities now agree it was recorded on 30 June 1950, a week before Navarro died from tuberculosis and heroin addiction. All the musicians are in great form, although the recording is poor. It has been suggested that this was Navarro's last effort, the flame burning brightest before the end. All are relaxed together for a change, and the set is a good example of a club date by some of the masters of be-bop.

The two other live recordings Powell made with Parker bracket what was effectively Powell's twenty-month absence from the scene from May 1951 to February 1953. The first comes from a radio broadcast from Birdland on 31 March 1951. The quintet is made up of Parker, Powell, Gillespie, Tommy Potter and Roy Haynes. The band is admirably recorded for the period and the musicians are excellent both individually and as a group. This is sparkling, first-rate bop, although there are slight signs that Powell is wavering. The musicians rattle through four bop classics: *Blue 'n' Boogie, Anthropology, 'Round Midnight* and *A Night In Tunisia*, together with a version of *Jumpin' With Symphony Sid*. The live broadcast contains the spoken introductions of the evening's compere, Sid Torin. Torin, better known as 'Symphony Sid', was the first radio disc-jockey to play the new music and became a renowned figure on the fringe of the scene. He seems unable to take charge of the proceedings here and suffers from Gillespie's irreverence. His lengthy introductions are pieces of inane hip chatter which come across as tediously irrelevant or as adding to the period charm and character of the date, according to the listener's mood.

This session dates from a time when the musicians were receiving less recognition than they had a few years before. Gillespie's big band had failed in 1950. He had turned to playing rhythm-and-blues influenced material for his own record company. Parker was recording, but often in commercialised settings such as with strings. Here, both are inventive and joyously extrovert, perhaps inspired by the fact that they were again playing their music in the right setting with the right people.

The second Parker–Powell collaboration was the concert in Toronto's Massey Hall on the night of 15 May 1953. Charles Mingus used an on-stage tape recorder to preserve for posterity the ideal group of bop players chosen by the members of the New Jazz Society of Toronto. Parker, Gillespie, Powell, Max Roach and Mingus himself formed the 'supergroup'.

Such special occasional gatherings of the great are usually disappointing, but not here. Despite the highly charged atmosphere and tensions, the music is excellent and the musicians are all involved and inspired – including Gillespie, who, in some of his playing of the period, was starting to exhibit the indifference and off-handedness that often marred his later career. Parker is almost overwhelmed by the flood of his ideas. On *A Night In Tunisia*, he cannot impose order on his imagination and his solo is a torrent of fragments. The quintet numbers generally consist of brief theme statements sandwiching a string of solos. Obviously there had been little or no rehearsal time, but the musicians had worked closely together in the past and their developments had not taken them far from the basic assumptions with which they started playing, so they easily fitted together again.

The original sleeve note of the Massey Hall tracks described Powell's playing as the 'unpredictable work of a madman', which is really a shameful inaccuracy. Drunk or not, he shows himself to be way above his many copyists. From the trio sides, *Cherokee* and *Lullaby Of Birdland* are taken at the fast tempos Powell loved, and are distinguished by changing interplay between his two hands, treble lines and harsh chords. *Sure Thing* is a very creative treatment of a popular melody. The concentrated *Jubilee* is of interest for the shadow of Teddy Wilson thrown over it.

In May 1949 Powell made the first of a number of trio sessions for Norman Granz with Roach and Ray Brown. This included *All God's Chillun Got Rhythm*, a favourite vehicle for Powell. Ira Gitler later remembered the impatience with which he and other enthusiasts waited for this set to appear. In many respects, the four sessions Powell made for Granz between 1949 and 1951 represent a peak of his recorded output. Hence we can consider these dates together: the first with Roach and Brown in May 1949; the second with Roach and Russell in January 1950; the third with Ray Brown and Buddy Rich in July 1950; and finally a set of solo piano from February 1951.

The May 1949 date is one of the most important sessions that Powell ever made. It was his first studio date for two years. During his absence from the studios, his powers had further improved. *Tempus Fugit, Chillun* and *Cherokee* show his overwhelming mastery of rapid tempos. His attack and flow of ideas are breathtaking examples of a sweeping, yet controlled imagination. The *Village Voice* critic Gary Giddins has described this version of *Cherokee* as 'one of those knucklebreaking ruminations played with fantastic precison'.

Tea For Two and *Hallelujah*, from July 1950, are similar fingerbreaking exercises. Powell races off in a torrent of notes. *Tea For Two* is one of his finest examples of pure technique at the fastest of tempos. Incidentally, Powell took an unusual amount of care with this track. He made ten takes before he was happy with the version originally issued on Clef 11069.

These, and the other rapid-fire tracks – *Just One Of Those Things* and *Get Happy* – perhaps focussed too much on his early skills. The impression he created, of great clarity and digital control, was so much identified with him that much of the best of his later work was under-rated because his dexterity was no longer so impressive, and he could not manage to maintain sustained choruses at such speeds. Max Harrison, in *The Essential Records*, sums up Powell's fast early recordings by observing that they contain '. . . the sort of headlong tempos in which only great executants are at ease, and, while the dazzling flow of ideas Powell throws off in these circumstances has often received comment, one cannot help wondering if non-pianists realise how demanding such improvising is in terms of physical energy and mental concentration, quite apart from the exorbitant rate at which musical ideas must be produced.'

The slow and medium-tempo numbers are of similar dramatic concentration to the fast numbers. Powell uses contrasting pianistic devices to reveal a comparable intensity of combined emotion and intellect. The slow ballads – such as the unaccompanied *Yesterdays* and *I'll Keep Loving You* – contrast touch and texture in chords, arpeggios, single-note lines, and the occasionally intrusive left hand that echoes the masters of stride. The medium-tempo numbers, such as *Strictly Confidential* and *Celia*, are diverse, and Powell occasionally resorts to double time to create further improvisational possibilities. *I'll Keep Loving You*, based on Richard Rodgers's *You Are Too Beautiful*, is deeply chorded and turns into a romantic offering, unusual from Powell. *Strictly Confidential* has light chords played in a style comparable to that popularised by George Shearing and is quite ethereal from so usually aggressive a pianist.

The January 1950 session is perhaps the least rewarding of the four. Here there are occasional lapses in time and realisation of ideas, as in *Sweet Georgia Brown*, where a Tatumesque run fails and Powell quickly reverts to the melody. At times his hands seem almost to knot up, an effect described with increasing frequency by those who witnessed his live performances over the following decade.

The final session is of extreme interest, as this contains eight unaccompanied solos offering a sustained view of the pianist alone. The first five numbers to be recorded are original compositions by Powell, and still strike the listener as fresh melodies. Apart from the extended *The Fruit*, all are exquisite miniatures running under two and a half minutes apiece. The other three titles from the date all recall Art Tatum in varying degrees. For virtually the last time, Powell's acknowledgement to stride appears: *The Last Time I Saw Paris* contains a full chorus (whether as a farewell, an affectionate commemoration or a humorous interjection can only be surmised). The shadow of Tatum stands over the harmonic and rhythmic devices used by Powell. *Just One Of Those Things* and *A Nightingale Sang* are typical Tatumesque *tours-de-force*, but the

language of the old master is rephrased by the modern master. Powell tears dramatically into the changes with a force that leaves any thought of Tatum behind. Powell was always to echo touches of the latter in his ballad work, yet it can be wondered if here he was trying to shake off the debt he owed.

On all the unaccompanied items Powell perhaps does little more than he would if bass and drums were present. The lack of accompaniment makes the left hand seem more prominent, and effectively destroys any argument that Powell was just a right-handed player.

Ten of the twenty-three numbers recorded on these four sessions are original compositions. As a general rule, his tunes have not been widely taken up by other musicians. It must be said that, where others have attempted them, Powell's themes have tended to lose something. Miles Davis tried *Tempus Fugit* in 1953 and made it sound like a technical exercise. Equally, Davis's version of *Hallucinations*, which he recorded as *Budo*, lacked the power of the composer's version. *Parisian Thoroughfare* was extensively and successfully featured by the Max Roach–Clifford Brown group, but owes much of its charm to the suggestion of moving traffic and a happy optimism which was typical of Brown.

Prior to the issue of the eagerly awaited trio recording of *All God's Chillun Got Rhythm*, Prestige issued a set recorded in December 1949 and January 1950 with Sonny Stitt, which included a version of this tune. On these recordings, Stitt plays tenor saxophone and is backed by Powell, Russell and Roach. According to Gene Lees, this was Stitt's first recording on tenor saxophone, which he had adopted in place of the alto to avoid criticisms that he was solely a Parker copyist. He had recorded in 1946 with Powell, with the Be-Bop Boys. Apparently, during the 1949 session Powell was on the receiving end of taunts from Stitt.

The taunting seems to have driven Powell and Stitt to greater effort. Both surpass themselves in invention and forceful swing. Powell plays on equal terms with Stitt, and as a soloist he could be considered to dominate the tenor saxophonist much of the time. Stitt, along with many other reed instrumentalists, has cited Powell as one of the main influences on his playing, together with Charlie Parker. It is significant, given the cohesion of this quartet, that its leaders were working regularly together that January, at the Orchid on 52nd Street.

In 1949, Powell made his first recordings for Blue Note. The first, in August, involved him in a quintet with the young Sonny Rollins, Fats Navarro, Tommy Potter and Roy Haynes. Several takes were made of the four full-band pieces from the session – *Wail, Dance Of The Infidels, Bouncin' With Bud* and *52nd St Theme*.

Powell and Navarro antagonised each other continually. Dizzy Gillespie has said of Navarro: 'Bud used to bug him all the time.' As a typical example of this, Leonard Feather has described events at a jam session at the Three Deuces: '. . . the tension between the two was aggravated as Bud chided Fats between sets. At the beginning of the next set Fats reached the bursting point. While the audience looked on in silent, terrified tension, he lifted his horn and tried to bring the full weight of it crashing down on Bud's hands. He missed, thank God, but the strength of the blow was enough to buckle the horn against the piano. Fats had to borrow a trumpet to play the set.' Feather adds, however, that the incident 'failed to affect the close friendship and mutual admiration between Bud and Fats'.

The tension between the two is evident on their Blue Note date, where they push each other to produce supreme examples of bop; the alternate takes are less polished than the ordered anger of the originally issued versions (these have 78 rpm issue numbers in the chronology). At the end of the session Powell recorded two trio tracks – *You Go To My Head* and *Ornithology*. Here the pressure between himself and Navarro had dissipated and Powell sounds drained. *You Go To My Head* is yet another echo of Art Tatum, and has something of a flawed ending.

Throughout the 1950s, Powell tended to work and record in a trio format (when he worked and recorded at all). He continued to make discs for three labels: Blue Note, Verve and Victor. The decade showed a continuing deterioration in his technical powers and facility of imagination. 1953 was the last year he was in full command of all his faculties as a pianist.

During the 1950s, Powell was at his most relaxed when playing for Blue Note. A comparison of alternate takes shows that he did not vary his performance drastically when perfecting a recording. *Night In Tunisia*, from May 1951, is offered in two takes which barely differ, except that the first has a rather hesitant close. The development of his latinesque piece *Un Poco Loco* can be traced over three takes. The first two are satisfactory and the third is a marginal improvement. Nevertheless, Powell was unhappy with the first take and stopped short, and the second is not really complete. The progression is interesting for the glimpses of Powell's mind at work, but shows nothing of the fundamental reworkings and re-appraisals that were demonstrated by Charlie Parker on his recordings for Savoy.

The August 1953 Blue Note date shows off Powell's new trio with George Duvivier on bass and Art Taylor on drums. These two subsequently made up Powell's trio for most of the mid-1950s. Duvivier's strong lines did much to hold the group together. Their numbers include Powell's bitter and harrowing *The Glass Enclosure*. The others show Powell in his now expected role of virtuoso, his brilliant technique displaying his complex, flowing ideas. His intensity turns to relaxation in the unusually easy-going *Collard Greens and Black-eyed Peas* (also known as *Blues In The Closet*).

In contrast to the Blue Note studio recordings, Powell can be heard in a live performance from Washington's Club Kavakos, taped earlier in 1953. It shows the pianist composed and assured

but not as meticulous as might be expected from his studio work. He was accompanied by Charles Mingus and Roy Haynes, and the evening was privately recorded by Bill Potts. There is some evidence of a decline in Powell's playing, as if his concentration was wandering and some of the chord sequences could not quite be recalled. The album containing this session, Elektra Musician K52363, also includes the interviews conducted with Powell by Henri Renaud and Francis Paudras, who translate the English questions and answers into French. Speculation on the dates of these appears in chapter five, but the sleeve suggests that the first interview was recorded at the sanatorium where Powell was recovering from tuberculosis. Powell sounds weak. His 'old man's' voice falters and he coughs as he answers what can only be regarded as simple questions about his music and his taste in musicians.

The sleeve note states that owing to Powell's weakness it was necessary to ask some questions several times before he was able to reply. In the first interview, he mentions that he has recently composed *In The Mood For A Classic*, a song written in hospital, he says, for France in general. Al Haig was his idea of the perfect pianist, but he always did like Billy Kyle, and later Hank Jones. Asked who was his piano teacher, Powell replies 'Art Tatum', and, asked if he spent much time with Tatum, he replies with the strange remarks: 'I don't know. Art Tatum used to take me out for a drive in his big Lincoln. He had a sky-blue Lincoln. I've been in his car.' Francis Paudras translates the French word *maître* as 'teacher'. Although this is one of its meanings, it really has the connotation of 'master', the one who leads for others to follow.

Later, Powell coughs weakly in answering that Monk was his preferred composer: 'one of my favourites from a long time ago. We used to hang out all day and all night at after-hours joints.' Asked about his other favourites, he mentions Johnny Griffin on sax, Miles Davis on trumpet, and Oscar Pettiford and Tommy Potter on bass, and says that his best-loved accompanists were Ray Brown and Max Roach.

The second interview is very short and took place later in a studio when Powell was well enough to be allowed out of the sanatorium for a few days.

He says he felt fine and that the doctors asserted he would be well soon and could go home. He still sounds weak and as though he does not believe what he says. He was finding the work of Charles Mingus and Toshiko (Akiyoshi) of interest and mentions that Art Tatum was 'still my best friend in music'. The interview ends with Powell stumbling over some French, like a child who has laboriously and uncertainly learnt a recitation: 'Bonsoir. Je reviens bientôt.'

Returning to Powell's earlier recordings, the series of sessions from his regular job at the Royal Roost in 1953 yield some good performances. Notable among them, from 14 February, is his trio with Roy Haynes and Oscar Pettiford, where Powell shows no lapses in either technique or concentration. The fast numbers are still fresh and crisp and alive, although, interestingly, the ballads sound below par, stale and dated.

As the 1950s went on, his recordings were to become poor offerings, often painful, at best uneven. There were good moments, but only moments. The music always had a kind of awesome power, since the listener, even if ignorant of Powell's story, is made fully aware of the inner tensions and struggles of the pianist. The total effect makes more emotional demands of the listener than the work of many lesser pianists whose talents remained unimpaired, but unimproved. One album, pointedly titled 'The Lonely One', was made up of tracks recorded for Norman Granz in January and April 1955 (Verve MGV8301). In his sleeve notes, Nat Hentoff sums up Powell's career at the time in one succinct paragraph: 'Bud's records are, in this respect, like his live appearances. They're not consistent. Some may be distorted in various ways throughout an entire album; some may come fully alive in sections; and a few in recent years have been sustained achievements.'

Of the Granz recordings from this period, up-tempo numbers – *Bean And The Boys, Lady Bird, Woody 'n' You, My Heart Stood Still* – only barely echo the old Powell, and those echoes carry none of his former brilliance and clarity. *Buttercup* strongly pre-figures much of the approach of the pianist Lennie Tristano. The Monk titles, *'Round Midnight* (December 1954) and *Epistrophy* (January 1955), are mediocre. Some tracks sound as if they are playing at half speed, while on *I Know That You Know* (September 1956) it is as if Powell's fingers are tangled. *Thou Swell* (January 1955) is a collection of fragments of unrealised lines of improvisations. On *Blues In The Closet* he appears to have lost all concentration and awareness of what he is doing. *It Never Entered My Mind* and *I Get A Kick Out Of You* are better conceived but still disappoint. Powell sounds here as though he should not be working, but resting and recovering. The recordings provide documentation of the period and are worthy of some study; casual listening suggests it might have been kinder for Powell not to have been recorded at all during these years.

In late 1956 and early 1957, Powell made two albums for Victor, 'Strictly Powell' and 'Swinging With Bud', both with Duvivier and Taylor. They were recorded before and after his tour of Europe with the 'Birdland' package in 1956. Both LPs show some improvement and are superior to the series of Blue Note albums recorded (1957– 8) before Powell went to France. He performs with some confidence and authority, and with fewer misfingerings. There is an atmosphere of calm in which Powell plays carefully, within his limits, keeping everything under what control he could exercise. Some of his right-handed lines approach his earlier work, as on *Elegy*, but he relies heavily on a two-handed chorded approach to convey his melancholia and self-pity. The music is subdued, unexcited. His range of tempos is narrow and unvaried. His articulation has lost its early bright clarity and tends to become blurred. It is music so far removed from his earlier recordings that it seems almost impossible that it could be the work of the same man. The steady playing of Duvivier holds it all together as the piano on the faster tempos sounds unstable.

On the Victor sessions Powell was still able to contribute some original compositions – *Elegy, Jump City, Topsy Turvy, Birdland Blues, Midway, Get It, Croscrane*. In his playing he nods at Tatum, recalls Shearing on *Lush Life*, is recklessly inaccurate on *Almost Like Being In Love*, loses rhythm with the dense chording of *They Didn't Believe Me* and *Blues For Bessie*, and, as ever, comes alive on the fast be-bop lines of *Shaw 'Nuff* and *Salt Peanuts*.

He made three albums for Blue Note between 1957 and the end of 1958 before leaving in 1959 for France. They were released as Volumes Three, Four and Five in 'The Amazing Bud Powell' sequence – 'Bud!', 'Time Waits', and 'The Scene Changes'. Overall, Powell sounds more at ease, remains thoughtful, but allows only a little of his old tense excitement to appear.

On 'Bud!', with Paul Chambers on bass and Art Taylor, and with trombonist Curtis Fuller on three tracks, Powell falters. *Frantic Fancies*, based on *Strike Up The Band*, lacks all authority and is a careless performance. He plays *Bud On Bach*, based on C. P. E. Bach's *Solfeggietto* which he had played as a child. He plays it straight before stepping into his improvisation and manages to make mistakes even with this simple piece. *Some Soul* prods at a slow blues in a manner reminiscent of Elmo Hope or other players who sought to imitate the young Powell.

'The Scene Changes' starts with four tracks in a minor key which all sound similar. The fifth track, *Borderick*, is an eight-bar nursery tune. The eight bars are repeated again and again with hardly any variation, speeding to what is almost a stride effect. A Latin number, *Comin' Up*, is played at length on the second side. This lasts for eight minutes and consists of rhythmic figures more suited to the work of a bored cocktail-bar pianist who has been asked to do a Latin number. The comparison with the earlier *Un Poco Loco* pointedly indicates Powell's decline in the eight years between the tracks. The effect of the album is of a dreamlike unreality.

The move to Paris was intended to benefit Powell, and on the evidence of his recordings, it did. He was in new surroundings, away from the hectic nightlife and temptations of New York and living in an ambience that respected the jazzman as an artist. His first recording more than bears this out, as well as justifying Jackie McLean's view that, during the Paris years, Powell pushed himself only at concerts: 'He plays a very commercial-type piano in the [Blue Note] club, but when he gets on a concert he really stretches out into fabulous Bud Powell, and you know he can be fabulous

Powell's April 1960 rhythm team of bassist Oscar Pettiford and drummer Kenny Clarke seen here with pianist Phineas Newborn.

when he wants to be. If you catch Bud at a concert over there, then you really get a chance to hear him.'

Powell sat in for half the album released as 'Blakey in Paris'. It was recorded at a concert at the Théâtre des Champs-Elysées in 1959 by the Art Blakey Jazz Messengers, with the addition of the young French tenorist Barney Wilen, and Powell sitting in part of the time for Walter Davis Jr. Two long versions of Powell's own *Dance Of The Infidels* and *Bouncin' With Bud* contain some of his best work since the early 1950s. Then he was able to conceive choruses as entities, building a performance from a succession of complete parts adding up to a full, logical progression. He almost regains this facility here.

He also performed well in the company of the old master Coleman Hawkins at the Essen Jazz Festival in April 1960. Hawkins fronts a trio of Powell, Oscar Pettiford and Kenny Clarke. There are also some trio tracks and a bass solo from Pettiford on *Willow Weep For Me*, together with a drum feature on

Salt Peanuts. Although Powell fumbles into the opening of *Shaw 'Nuff*, the bop standard which was a favourite of his during these years, on the other tracks he sounds relaxed and produces some of the best work of his late style – spare, terse, and above all controlled. *Shaw 'Nuff* gallops at eighty bars to the minute. Powell holds the tempo but his ideas cannot quite match this speed and his touch is unsure. On *Blues In The Closet* and *John's Abbey* he improves; the bop runs are articulated cleanly but are not fully rounded or completed as if not absolutely thought through. The bleak arpeggios of Coleman Hawkins provoke a better response from Powell than the old boys' reunion with Dexter Gordon and Kenny Clarke three years later was to produce.

Oscar Pettiford had been a European resident since 1958, when he came over from the States as part of a 'Jazz From Carnegie Hall'

Clarke, Michelot and Powell.

package. Five months after the Essen set he was dead. His place in the trio was taken by the French bassist Pierre Michelot. The new trio recorded live, again at the Théâtre des Champs-Elysées, in October 1960 at a memorial concert for Pettiford. The four tracks – *Buttercup, John's Abbey, Sweet And Lovely* and *Crossin' The Channel* – catch Powell on a good night. Slightly uneven, he improvises fluently. *Channel* has him in a flood of his characteristic be-bop runs.

The Pettiford memorial tracks appear on a Xanadu album which is a collection of Powell's playing from the period 1959–60, including tracks by the trio and a duo of Powell and Johnny Griffin, as well as a set with Barney Wilen and the trio. The contest with the exuberant Griffin produces the best music. This album, the Hawkins set and the side with Blakey make up the best of Powell's last recordings.

The Michelot–Clarke trio were recorded again, in 1961, on 'At The Blue Note Cafe' (ESP1066). This is an uneasy and unsatisfying set. Powell's runs are incomplete, fingerings are missed, and for much of the album, his concentration is absent. The opener, *There Will Never Be Another You*, is diffident to the point of lethargy. Powell's chording here barely rises above that of an indifferent cocktail-bar pianist. He sounds interested on *Thelonious*, an up-tempo number, where the bass and drums work hard to prod him into Monkish single notes and spacings. He does little with *'Round Midnight* and meanders to such an extent on *Monk's Mood* that the issued version clearly stops when the tape has been cut short. The set is comprised of standard bop numbers – such as *Lover Man, Shaw 'Nuff* and *Night In Tunisia*. Even these tunes do not inspire him as they usually do. The one non-standard bop tune is *There Will Never Be Another You*. This was often used by Powell as the last number of the evening, perhaps as a cynical aside for the benefit of the audience.

Powell toured Scandinavia in early 1962, and too many recordings were issued from his sessions at the Golden Circle in Stockholm. Poor drumming in Stockholm and, later, in Copenhagen did nothing to help Powell, although he benefits from the bass playing of the fifteen-year-old Niels-Henning Ørsted Pedersen in Copenhagen.

Five albums were issued on Steeplechase from the Stockholm sessions. A condensation to two albums by reasonable selection would have left a kinder memorial to Powell's work of the time, but what survives is poor and downright tedious, as the sixty or so choruses of *Straight No Chaser* proves. The Copenhagen set came out as 'Bouncing With Bud', and captures the final best moments Powell put down on record. It consists mainly of bop standards, the standards of Powell's youth and early maturity which nearly always seemed to revive some of his past talent. To compare this version of *Bouncin' With Bud* with the 1949 recording is unfair. The staggering virtuosity of the youth of 1949 is long dead, and replaced by a tired, worn-out man. On 'Bouncing With Bud' Powell is relaxed as though he has fully accepted his life and circumstances. The recording suggests worldly experience without self-pity. The version of *I Remember Clifford* is beautiful, but it is a sad reminder of things lost. The once all-powerful and dominant piano allows Ørsted Pedersen to carry the line of the tune on the bass.

Powell's regular trio with Clarke and Michelot appear on 'A Portrait Of Thelonious', made in December 1961. This set was recorded in a Paris studio and supervised by Cannonball Adderley. Although it is claimed it was recorded 'live', the applause has been added afterwards. Half the numbers are not by Monk. Powell treats his old colleague with respect, basing his improvisation on Monk's melodies and not solely on the chord sequences. To some extent, he dispenses with what remains of his own style and immerses himself in Monk's world. Even though the association with Thelonious gives these tunes some inspiration, and even

'Our man in Paris' – Dexter Gordon as he appeared in Bertrand Tavernier's film – 'Round Midnight', which was partly based on 'La Danse de Infidèles'.

though Powell may have been amongst the best interpreters of Monk's themes, this set can only be called average.

Eighteen months or so later, Dexter Gordon made an album with the trio, but generally this, too, is a disappointment. Issued as 'Our Man In Paris', it marked the beginning of the revival of Gordon's career. At that time, Gordon, like Powell, was based in Paris. The music is good and competent, but no one plays with any real fire. The whole session is controlled by Clarke. Powell plays with care, paring his work down to a simple, well-organised and restrained lyricism.

The 1964 set initially issued as 'Blues For Bouffemont' has Powell accompanied by Michel Gaudry on bass and Art Taylor on drums. It was recorded in Paris just prior to Bud's return to New York. *Bouffemont*, a rarity for Powell, is a slow blues, and named after the French sanatorium where he recovered from tuberculosis. The blues coaxes a response from the listener through Powell's emotional involvement, although his fumbled, simple fingerings and stabbing block chords could almost be the first attempts at improvisation by a novice. The numbers with bop associations – *Little Willie Leaps, Moose The Mooche, My Old Flame*, and Parker's tribute to one of his stays in hospital after his West Coast breakdown, *Relaxin' At Camarillo* – also have a moving quality. Powell seems unable to keep up with fast tempos and his ideas do not flow. Any idea has to be dwelt on and carefully developed. There are flashes of the old brilliance and he tries to open up on the faster tempos which used to sustain and inspire him. He lacks the co-ordination to bring cohesion to this faster work and plays his runs as though working out in advance whether he will be able to finish them. *In The Mood For A Classic* and *Una Noche Con Francis* are two Powell compositions which date from his hospitalisation in Paris. Both are surprisingly strong, even if *Noche* comes from a standard be-bop riff based on *Perdido*.

The session for Roulette with John Ore on bass and J. G. Moses on drums made just after Powell's return to New York is quite dreadful. He stumbles and falters throughout, a faint echo of his old self, and, to some extent, even a parody of his late self. The session is so poor, the tape should have been destroyed and never considered for commercial release.

Any musician's work is necessarily studied chronologically. For many jazzmen, the time-span from emergence to maturity tends to be short. And for most of the prime movers in the bop movement, their period of maturity and dominance averages about seven years. The majority matured early, announced the new message, and then went on to rework that message rather than to renew themselves and their ideas.

This survey of his recordings reinforces the view that from 1947 to 1953 Powell was the supreme jazz pianist. These mature years produced some of the most startling piano ever recorded. Most of the best of his high-speed linear improvisations build towards a continuous driving climax. His lines would be based on a tune's chordal structure but flowed independently of it. In his best solos, Powell was uninhibited by the harmonic unit of a piece. He relied less on structure than on a seemingly endless flow of ideas. Even at headlong speed, he demonstrated an extraordinary supple and subtle rhythmic grasp, greater than that of Art Tatum, whose shadow nevertheless stands over much of Powell's work. The tension he generated was all his own. The effect of both his hands working together in his best recordings is like a trumpet or saxophone improvising over a supporting piano accompaniment.

Much of this effect was gained by formidable concentration and single-mindedness. Powell's untiring urgency and attack made

Opposite and right: two shots of Powell from his Paris period.

tremendous demands on his emotion and intellect. Technique, feelings and ideas were so delicately balanced in his playing that it was inevitable that he was unable to hold them together.

Sadly, he was to lose his fluency and imagination. Apart from a few late flowerings, the loss proved to be permanent. Ira Gitler once described him as 'a man walking a tightrope over a chasm of poetic beauty and madness.' The story of Powell's life and his work encourage such effusive wordplay, yet Gitler's phrase is as good a summary as any of his early work. Nevertheless Powell could not walk the tightrope for very long, and his decline began in earnest in 1953. He would never again surpass or even rival the speed and articulation of Tatum. He was often to descend into mediocrity, even painful incompetence, and he took refuge in simpler techniques. The greatest tragedy of Powell's final years is that even when he played badly, the listener can sense his unique mind and talent at work.

Only rarely was Bud Powell able to leave a record of his complete powers. The handful of discs from the late 1940s and early 1950s – the 1947 Roost sessions, the first two Blue Notes, the early Verves, the tracks with Parker and Stitt – give us a clear impression of what Bud Powell was. These recordings alone show why he was to be a dominant influence on the pianists who followed, and they confirm his standing as one of the greatest of all jazz musicians.

RECORDING CHRONOLOGY
COMPILED BY ALYN SHIPTON

This chronology is intended to help underpin Powell's career with a clear statement of known recording dates. The editor would like to acknowledge help from Barry Kernfeld, and from the librarian and staff of the British Sound Archive. The following works have been consulted, as well as other publications cited in the full bibliography:

Walter Bruyninckx: *Sixty Years of Recorded Jazz* ([Mechelen, Belgium, 1978–80])

Walter Bruyninckx: *Modern Jazz Discography* ([Mechelen, Belgium, 1984–])

Michael Cuscuna and Michael Ruppli: *The Blue Note Label: A Discography* (Westport, CT, 1988)

Michael Frohne: *Subconscious-Lee: 35 Years of Records and Tapes: The Lee Konitz Discography, 1947–82* (Freiburg, Germany, 1983)

Deiter Hartman: *Discography of Cootie Williams* (Basel, Switzerland, 1960) [special issue of *Jazz Statistics*]

Ralph Laing and Chris Sheridan: *Jazz Records: The Specialist Labels* (Copenhagen, 1981)

David Meeker: *Jazz in the Movies* (London, 1981)

Brian Priestley: *Mingus: A Critical Biography* (London, 1982)

Brian Priestley: *Charlie Parker* (Tunbridge Wells, 1984)

Michael Ruppli with Bob Porter: *The Prestige Label: A Discography* (Westport, CT, 1980)

Michael Ruppli with Bob Porter: *The Savoy Label: A Discography* (Westport, CT, 1980)

Claude Schlouch: *Once Upon a Time: Bud Powell – A Discography* (Marseille, 1983)

Abbreviations:

alt	alternative take	gtr	guitar
arr	arranger	pno	piano
as	alto saxophone	sbs	string bass
bar	baritone saxophone	tmb	trombone
clt	clarinet	tpt	trumpet
cond	conductor	ts	tenor saxophone
dm	drums	v	vocal

Bud Powell (pno) appears on every track; other personnel and instruments are given where known. First issue details only are included.

4 January 1944. NYC
Cootie Williams Sextet: Williams (tpt, v); Eddie Vinson (as, v); Eddie 'Lockjaw' Davis (ts); Norman Keenan (sbs); Sylvester 'Vess' Payne (dm)

CR345	You Talk A Little Trash (vEV)	Hit 8089
CR346	Floogie Boo (vEV)	—
CR347	I Don't Know	Hit 8090
CR348	Gotta Do Some War Work Baby (vCW)	—

6 January 1944. NYC
Cootie Williams Sextet: as 4 January

CR349	My Old Flame	Hit 8087
CR350	Sweet Lorraine	Hit 8088
CR351	Echoes Of Harlem	Hit 8087
CR352	Honeysuckle Rose	Hit 8088

Same date
Cootie Williams Orchestra: as Sextet, plus Ermit V. Perry, George Treadwell, Harold 'Money' Johnson (tpt); Ed Burke, George Stevenson, Bob Horton (tmb); Charlie Holmes (as); Lee Pope (ts); Eddie de Verteuil (bar; Pearl Bailey (v)

CR353	Now I Know (vPB)	Hit 7075
CR354	Tess's Torch Song (vPB)	—
CR355	Cherry Red Blues (vEV)	Hit 7084
CR356	Things Ain't What They Used To Be (vEV)	—

? May 1944. Hollywood
Cootie Williams Orchestra: Williams (tpt); Vinson (as); Sam 'The Man' Taylor (ts); rest unidentified (film soundtrack)

Theme	Extreme Rarities 1002
Wild Fire	—

2 May 1944. Hollywood
Cootie Williams Orchestra: Williams, Perry, Treadwell, Lammar Wright Sr, Tommy Stevenson (tpt); Burke, Horton, Ed Glover (tmb); Charlie Parker, Rupert Cole, Frank Powell (as); Taylor, Pope (ts); de Verteuil (bar); Leroy Kirkland (gtr); Carl Pruitt (sbs); Payne (dm)

Air Mail Special	Connoisseur Rarities 522
Roll 'em	—
The Boppers (sextet)*	—

*Some sources give this sextet as **Late 1944, Savoy Ballroom, NYC (Airshot)**

22 August 1944. NYC
Cootie Williams Orchestra: Williams, Perry, Treadwell, Wright,

Stevenson (tpt); Burke, Horton, Glover, Dan Logan (tmb); Vinson, Powell (as); Taylor, Pope (ts); de Verteuil (bar); Kirkland (gtr); Pruitt (sbs); Payne (dm)

T448	Is You Is Or Is You Ain't (vEV)	Hit 7108
T449	Somebody's Gotta Go (vEV)	Hit 7119
T450	'Round Midnight	—
T451	Blue Garden Blues	Hit 7108

2 May 1945. NYC
Frank Socolow's Duke Quintet: Freddy Webster (tpt); Socolow (ts); Leonard Gaskin (sbs); Irv Kluger (dm)

	The Man I Love	Duke 112
	Reverse The Charges	—
	Blue Fantasy	Duke 115
	September In The Rain	—

29 January 1946. NYC
Dexter Gordon Quintet: Leonard Hawkins (tpt); Gordon (ts); Curly Russell (sbs); Max Roach (dm)

S5878	Long Tall Dexter	Savoy 603
S5878	Long Tall Dexter (alt)	Savoy SJL 2211
S5879-1	Dexter Rides Again	Savoy 623
S5880-7	I Can't Escape From You (alt)	Savoy SJL 2211
S5880-13	I Can't Escape From You	Savoy 595
S5881	Dexter Digs In	Savoy 595, 603
S5881	Dexter Digs In (alt)	Savoy SJL 2211

7 May 1946. NYC
Sarah Vaughan with Tadd Dameron's Orchestra: Vaughan (v); Dameron (cond/arr); Freddy Webster (tpt); Leroy Harris (as); Leo Parker (bar); Ted Sturgis (sbs); Kenny Clarke (dm); plus 9 strings (unidentified)

5485	If You Could See Me Now	Musicraft 380
5486	I Could Make You Love Me	Musicraft 398
5487	You're Not The Kind	Musicraft 380
5488	My Kinda Love	Musicraft 398
5488	My Kinda Love (alt)	Vernon MVM 504

26 June 1946. NYC
Jay Jay Johnson's Be-Boppers: Johnson (tmb); Cecil Payne (as); Leonard Gaskin (sbs); Max Roach (dm)

S3309-1	Jay Bird	Savoy SJL 2232
S3309-9	Jay Bird	—
S3309-11	Jay Bird	Savoy 975
S3310-1	Coppin' The Bop	Savoy 615
S3311-1	Jay Jay	Savoy SJL 2232
S3311-2	Jay Jay	Savoy 615
S3311-4	Jay Jay	Savoy SJL 2232
S3312-1	Mad Be Bop	Savoy 930

23 August 1946. NYC
Sonny Stitt Be-Bop Boys*: Kenny Dorham (tpt); Stitt (as); Al Hall (sbs); Wallace Bishop(dm)

S3338	Bebop In Pastel (Bouncin' With Bud)	Savoy XP 8045
S3338	Bebop In Pastel (alt)	Savoy SJL 2247
S3339	Fool's Fancy (Wail)	Savoy XP 8044
S3340	Bombay	—
S3341A	Ray's Idea	Savoy 619

Kenny Clarke (dm) replaces Bishop

S3342	Serenade To A Square	Savoy 940
S3343A	Good Kick	Savoy 619
S3344	Seven Up	Savoy 930
S3345	Blues In Bebop	Savoy 978
S3345	Blues In Bebop (Blues À La Bud) (alt)	Savoy XP 8097
	Diz-iz	Savoy XP 8098

*The tracks with Bishop are sometimes identified as by Sonny Stitt's All-Stars, and sometimes as the Be-Bop Boys under Kenny Dorham's leadership. The tracks with Clarke are usually identified as solely under Stitt's leadership.

5 September 1946. NYC
Kenny Clarke: Fats Navarro, Kenny Dorham (tpt); Sonny Stitt (as); Ray Abrams (ts); Eddie de Verteuil (bar); John Collins (gtr); Al Hall (sbs); Clarke (dm); Walter Fuller (arr)

D6VB2792-1	Epistrophy	Swing 224
D6VB2793-1	52nd St Theme	Swing 244
D6VB2794-1	Oop Bop Sh-bam	Swing 224
D6VB2795-1	Rue Chaptal (Royal Roost)	Swing 244

6 September 1946. NYC
Be-Bop Boys (also known as Fats Navarro/Gil Fuller's Modernists): Kenny Dorham, Fats Navarro (tpt); Sonny Stitt (as); Morris Lane (ts); Eddie de Verteuil (bar); Al Hall (sbs); Kenny Clarke (dm)

S3346	Boppin' A Riff I	Savoy 588
S3347	Boppin' A Riff II	—
S3348	Fat Boy I	Savoy 587
S3349	Fat Boy II	—
S3350	Everything's Cool I	Savoy 586
S3351	Everything's Cool II	—
S3352	Webb City I	Savoy 585
S3353	Webb City II	—

10 January 1947. NYC
Bud Powell Trio: Curly Russell (sbs); Max Roach (dm)

2991	I'll Remember April	Roost 513
2992	Indiana	Roost 518
2993	Somebody Loves Me	Roost 509

2994	I Should Care	Roost 521
2995	Bud's Bubble	Roost 509
2996	Off Minor	Roost 513
2997	Nice Work If You Can Get It	Roost 521
2998	Everything Happens To Me	Roost 518

4 May 1947. NYC

Charlie Parker All Stars: Miles Davis (tpt); Parker (as); Tommy Potter (sbs); Max Roach (dm)

S3420-1	Donna Lee	Savoy SJL 5500
S3420-2	Donna Lee	Savoy MG 12001
S3420-3	Donna Lee	Savoy MG1200
S3420-4	Donna Lee	Savoy MG 12009
S3420-5	Donna Lee	Savoy 652
S3421-1	Chasing the Bird	Savoy MG 12001
S3421-2	Chasing the Bird	Savoy SJL 5500
S3421-3	Chasing the Bird	Savoy MG 12009
S3421-4	Chasing the Bird	Savoy 977
S3422-1	Cheryl	Savoy MG 12001
S3422-2	Cheryl	Savoy 952
S3423-1	Buzzy	Savoy MG 12009
S3423-2	Buzzy	Savoy MG 12001
S3423-3	Buzzy	—
S3423-4	Buzzy	Savoy MG 12000
S3423-5	Buzzy	Savoy 652

19 December 1948. NYC

'Great Jazz Concerts at the Original Royal Roost': Benny Harris (tpt); J. J. Johnson (tmb); Buddy de Franco (clt); Lee Konitz (as); Budd Johnson (ts); Cecil Payne (bar); Chuck Wayne (gtr); Nelson Boyd (sbs); Max Roach (dm); Leonard Feather (announcer)

	Perdido	WMTM broadcast (unissued)
	Indiana	—
	All The Things You Are*	—
	Jumpin' With Symphony Sid	Beppo BEP503
	I'll Be Seeing You	—
	52nd St Theme	—
	Ornithology	—

*Konitz does not play on 1st three tracks; *no brass or reeds; Barbara Carroll (pno) added*

7 May 1949. NYC

Bud Powell Trio: Ray Brown (sbs); Max Roach (dm)

C 242-1	Tempus Fugit	Clef 11045
C 243-1	Celia	Clef 11046
C 244-1	Cherokee	Clef EPC 4007
C 245-1	I'll Still Keep Loving You (pno solo)	Clef 11045

C 246-1	Strictly Confidential	Clef 11047
C 247-1	All God's Chillun Got Rhythm	Clef 11046

Michael Ruppli suggests these were recorded in February 1949.

8 August 1949*. NYC
Bud Powell's Modernists/Trio: Fats Navarro (tpt); Sonny Rollins (ts); Tommy Potter (sbs); Roy Haynes (dm)

BN 360-0	Bouncin' With Bud	Blue Note BLP 1532
BN 360-1	Bouncin' With Bud	Blue Note BLP 1532
BN 360-2	Bouncin' With Bud	Blue Note 1567
BN 361-0	Wail	Blue Note BLP 1531
BN 361-3	Wail	Blue Note 1567
BN 362-0	Dance Of The Infidels	Blue Note BLP 1532
BN 362-1	Dance Of The Infidels	Blue Note 1568
BN 363-1	52nd St Theme	—
BN 364	You Go To My Head (trio)	Blue Note 1566
BN 365-0	Ornithology (trio)	—
BN 365-1	Ornithology (trio)	Blue Note BLP 1504

Items on this list without the prefix BLP are original 78 rpm issues, and should not be confused with the LP series despite similar numbering.
*Some Blue Note reissue sleeve notes give 9 August for this session.

11 December 1949. NYC
Sonny Stitt Quartet: Stitt (ts); Curly Russell (sbs); Max Roach (dm)

JRC1000A	All God's Chillun Got Rhythm	Prestige 705
JRC1001	Sonny Side	Prestige 722
JRC1002B	Bud's Blues	Prestige 706
JRC1003A	Sunset	Prestige 705

19 December 1949. NYC
Incorrect dating for Royal Roost Broadcast of 19 December 1948, included in some published sources.

24 December 1949. Carnegie Hall, NYC
Bud Powell Trio: Curly Russell (sbs); Max Roach (dm)

	All God's Chillun Got Rhythm	IAJRC 20

Same, plus Miles Davis (tpt); Sonny Stitt (as); Benny Green (tmb); Serge Chaloff (bar)

	Move	IAJRC 20
	Hot House	—
	Ornithology (incomplete)	—

? January 1950. NYC
Bud Powell Trio: Curly Russell (sbs); Max Roach (dm)

C 341-2	So Sorry, Please	Clef 11060
C 342-2	Get Happy	Clef 11061
C 343-1	Sometimes I'm Happy	—
C 344-2	Sweet Georgia Brown	Clef 11059
C 345-1	Yesterdays (pno solo)	Clef 11047

| C 346-1 | April In Paris | Clef 11060 |
| C 347-1 | Body And Soul | Clef 11059 |

Michael Ruppli suggests this took place in February 1950.

26 January 1950. NYC
Sonny Stitt Quartet: as 11 December 1949

JRC1004D	Strike Up The Band	Prestige 758
JRC1005B	I Want To Be Happy	—
JRC1006D	Taking A Chance On Love	Prestige 722
JRC1007A	Fine And Dandy	Prestige 706
JRC1007B	Fine And Dandy (alt)	Prestige PRLP 7024

17 or 30 June 1950. Birdland, NYC (Airshot)
Charlie Parker Quintet: Fats Navarro (tpt); Parker (as); Curly Russell (sbs); Art Blakey (dm)

Night In Tunisia (Parker out)	CBS 88250
Out Of Nowhere	Ozone 9
Embraceable You (unknown v)	[no details]
Cool Blues (introduces)	CPR 701A
52nd St Theme (I)	—
Move (introduces)	—
52nd St Theme (II)	Ozone 9
The Street Beat (introduces)	CPR 701B
52nd St Theme (III)	Ozone 4
Perdido	CPR 701B
Round Midnight (Navarro out)	CPR 701A
Dizzy Atmosphere	Ozone 4
This Time The Dream's On Me (Navarro out)	Ozone 4
Little Wille Leaps (introduces)	Meexa Discox 1776
52nd St Theme (IV)	—
I'll Remember April (Navarro out, introduces)	CBS 88250
52nd St Theme (V)	—
Ornithology	CPR 701A

The word 'introduces' designates pieces which finish by leading directly into 52nd St Theme with no break. There is a very confused issue history of this session. The clearest statement of events is in P. Koster and D. Bakker: Charlie Parker: i-iv (1974-6) [discography].

? July 1950. NYC
Bud Powell Trio: Ray Brown (sbs); Buddy Rich (dm)

C 435-6	Hallelujah	Clef 11069
C 436-5	Tea For Two	Norgran MGN 1036
C 436-6	Tea For Two	Clef MGC 610
C 436-10	Tea For Two	Clef 11069

? February 1951. NYC
Bud Powell (solo pno)

C 571-1	Parisian Thoroughfare	Clef MGC 610
C 572-1	Oblivion	—
C 573-1	Dusk At Sandi	—
C 574-5	Hallucinations	—
C 575-2	The Fruit	—
C 576-1	A Nightingale Sang In Berkeley Square	—
C 577-2	Just One Of Those Things	—
C 578-1	The Last Time I Saw Paris	—

31 March 1951. Birdland, NYC
Dizzy Gillespie/Charlie Parker Quintet: Gillespie (tpt); Parker (as); Tommy Potter (sbs); Roy Haynes (dm)

	Blue 'n' Boogie	Temple M555
	Anthropology	—
	'Round Midnight	—
	A Night In Tunisia	—
	Jumpin' With Symphony Sid	—

1 May 1951. NYC
Bud Powell Trio: Curly Russell (sbs); Max Roach (dm)

BN 382-1	Un Poco Loco (alt 1)	Blue Note BLP 1503
BN 382-2	Un Poco Loco (alt 2)	—
BN 382-4	Un Poco Loco	Blue Note 1577
BN 383-0	Over The Rainbow (pno solo)	Blue Note 1576
BN 384-0	Night In Tunisia	—
BN 384-1	Night In Tunisia (alt)	Blue Note BLP 1503
BN 385-0	It Could Happen To You (pno solo, alt)	—
BN 385-1	It Could Happen To You (pno solo)	Blue Note 1577
	Parisian Thoroughfare	Blue Note BLP 1503

7 February 1953. Royal Roost, NYC (Airshot)
Bud Powell Trio: Oscar Pettiford (sbs); Roy Haynes (dm)

	Tea For Two	Alto AL 715
	It Could Happen To You	—
	Lover Come Back To Me	—

14 February 1953. Royal Roost, NYC (Airshot)
Bud Powell Trio: Pettiford (sbs); Haynes (dm)

	Lullaby Of Birdland	Alto AL715
	I Want To Be Happy	—
	Embraceable You	—
	I've Got You Under My Skin	—
	Ornithology	—

7 March 1953. Royal Roost, NYC (Airshot)
Bud Powell Trio: Franklin Skeete (sbs); Sonny Payne (dm)

Lullaby Of Birdland	(unissued)
Hallelujah	Alto AL715
How High The Moon	—
Hallucinations (Budo)	Queen-Disc Q-024
I've Got You Under My Skin	Base 3033
Embraceable You	—
Lullaby Of Birdland	—

14 March 1953. NYC (Airshot)
Bud Powell Trio: Skeete (sbs); Payne (dm)

Sure Thing	Session Disc LP109

21 March 1953. NYC (Airshot)
Bud Powell Trio: Charles Mingus (sbs); Roy Haynes (dm)

I Want To Be Happy	Session Disc LP109
I've Got You Under My Skin	—
Embraceable You	—
Woody 'n' You	—
Salt Peanuts	—

5 April 1953. Club Kavakos, Washington, DC (Airshot/live recording)
Bud Powell Trio: Mingus (sbs); Haynes (dm)

I Want To Be Happy	Elektra Musician E1-60030
Somebody Loves Me	—
Nice Work If You Can Get It	—
Salt Peanuts	—
Conception	—
Lullaby Of Birdland	—
Little Willie Leaps	—
Hallelujah	—
Lullaby Of Birdland (alt)	—
Sure Thing	—
Woody 'n' You	—

15 May 1953. Massey Hall, Toronto
Bud Powell Trio: Charles Mingus (sbs); Max Roach (dm)

Cherokee	Debut DLP 3
Embraceable You	—
Jubilee	—
Sure Thing	—
Lullaby Of Birdland	—
I've Got You Under My Skin	Debut DLP 198
Bass-ically Speaking	(unissued)

Same date. Same venue
Quintet of the Year: as above, plus Charlie Parker (as); Dizzy Gillespie
(tpt)

Perdido	Debut DLP 2

All The Things You Are	—
Salt Peanuts	—
Wee	Debut DLP 4
Hot House	—
A Night In Tunisia	—

? May 1953. Toronto
Dizzy Gillespie Quartet: as Quintet of the Year, minus Parker

Woody 'n' You	Duke D1019

? May 1953. NYC (Airshot)
Charlie Parker Quartet: Parker (as); Mingus (sbs); Roach (dm)

Dance Of The Infidels	Parktec 4627-1

22 May 1953. Birdland, NYC
Charlie Parker Quartet: Parker (as); Mingus (sbs); Art Taylor (dm)

Cool Blues	(unissued)
All The Things You Are	—
Lullaby Of Birdland	—

According to Schlouch, a tape exists of this airshot.

30 May 1953. Birdland, NYC (Airshot)
Charlie Parker Quintet: Parker (as); Mingus (sbs); Taylor (dm); Candido Camera (conga)

Moose The Mooche	Queen Disc 002
Cheryl	—
Lullaby Of Birdland	—

Same date. Same venue (Airshot)
Bud Powell Trio: as above, without Parker, Camera

I've Got You Under My Skin	Base 3034
Autumn In New York	Session Disc LP109
I Want To Be Happy	—

4 June 1953. NYC
Bud Powell Trio: Mingus (sbs); Taylor (dm)

Moose The Mooche	Base 3034

20 June 1953. NYC
Bud Powell Trio: Mingus (sbs); Taylor (dm)

Budo (Hallucinations)	Queen Disc 024
My Heart Stood Still	—
Dance Of The Infidels	Session Disc 109
Lullaby Of Birdland	—

Some sources give George Duvivier (sbs) in place of Mingus for this broadcast.

11 July 1953. Birdland, NYC (Airshot)
Bud Powell Trio: Mingus (sbs); Taylor (dm)

	Budo	(unissued)
	My Heart Stood Still	—
	Dance Of The Infidels	Base 3034

There is much duplication of repertory here, and quite possibly some misattribution and dating. Some of the details of Base 3034 seem particularly suspect.

26 July 1953. Open Door Club, NYC
Charlie Parker Quintet
Powell appears on some tracks of this extant but unissued session, on which Al Haig also plays piano.

14 August 1953. WOR Studios, NYC
Bud Powell Trio: George Duvivier (sbs); Art Taylor (dm)

BN510-6	Autumn In New York	Blue Note BLP 5041
BN509-1	Reets And I	—
BN509-2	Reets And I	Blue Note BST84430
BN511-2	Sure Thing	Blue Note 1629
BN512-0	Collard Greens And Black-eyed Peas (alt)	Blue Note BST84430
BN512-2	Collard Greens And Black-eyed Peas	Blue Note 1629
BN513-0	Polka Dots And Moonbeams	Blue Note BLP 5041
BN514-1	I Want To Be Happy	Blue Note 1628
BN515-1	Audrey	Blue Note BLP 5041
BN516-0	The Glass Enclosure	Blue Note 1628
BN517-0	I've Got You Under My Skin	(rejected)

The initial matrices for this session were reversed, and represent takes 8 and 9 respectively.

? September 1953. NYC
Bud Powell Trio: Duvivier (sbs); Taylor (dm)

	Embraceable You	Roost LP412
	Burt Covers Bud	—
	Bag's Groove	—
	My Devotion	—
	Stella By Starlight (pno solo)	—
	My Heart Stood Still	—
	Woody 'n' You	—
	You'd Be So Nice To Come Home To	—

? September 1953, NYC
Bud Powell Trio: Duvivier (sbs); Taylor (dm)

	My Devotion	Fantasy 6006
	Polka Dots And Moonbeams	—
	My Heart Stood Still	—
	I Want To Be Happy	—

5 September 1953. Birdland, NYC (Airshot)
Bud Powell Trio: Duvivier (sbs); Taylor (dm)

Lullaby Of Birdland	(unissued)
My Heart Stood Still	Base 3035
Un Poco Loco	—
Parisian Thoroughfare	Queen Disc Q-024
Dance Of The Infidels	Base 3035
Glass Enclosure	Queen Disc Q-024

Some sources give Roach as the drummer on these tracks.

19 September 1953. Birdland, NYC (Airshot)
Bud Powell Trio: Duvivier (sbs); Taylor (dm)

Parisian Thoroughfare	Base 3035
Dance Of The Infidels	—

Same date. Same venue
Bud Powell Trio: Curly Russell replaces Duvivier

Un Poco Loco	Base 3035
Oblivion	—

26 September 1953. Birdland, NYC (Airshot)
Bud Powell Trio: Russell (sbs); Taylor (dm)

Parisian Thoroughfare	Base 3035
Dance Of The Infidels	—
Embraceable You	—
Un Poco Loco	—
Oblivion	—
Lullaby Of Birdland	(unissued)

2 June 1954. NYC
Bud Powell Trio: Percy Heath (sbs)*; Taylor (dm)

1726-2	Moonlight In Vermont	Norgran EPN 41
1727-1	Spring Is Here	—
1728-1	Buttercup	—
1729-3	Fantasy In Blue	—

4 June 1954. NYC
Bud Powell Trio: Heath (sbs)*; Taylor (dm)

1760-1	It Never Entered My Mind	Norgran MGN 23
1761-3	A Foggy Day	—
1762-1	Time Was	—
1763-1	My Funny Valentine	—

*Michael Ruppli suggests the bassist on both these sessions is George Duvivier.

16 December 1954. NYC
Bud Powell Trio: Heath (sbs); Max Roach (dm)

2138-4	Like Someone In Love	
	(pno solo)	Norgran EPN 94

2139-1	Deep Night	Norgran EPN 93
2140-1	Old Black Magic	—
2140-3	Old Black Magic (alt)	Verve VE2 2526
2141-1	'Round Midnight	—

11 January 1955. NYC
Bud Powell Trio: Lloyd Trotman (sbs); Art Blakey (dm)

2154-2	Thou Swell	Norgran EPN 94
2155-2	Someone To Watch Over Me	—
2156-1	Lover Come Back To Me	Norgran EPN 95
2157-2	Tenderly	—

12 January 1955. NYC
Bud Powell Trio: as 11 January

2158	How High The Moon	Norgran EPN 95
2159-2	I Get A Kick Out Of You	MGN 1064
2159-3	I Get A Kick Out of You	Verve VE2 2526
2160	You Go To My Head	Norgran MGN 1064
2161	The Best	—

13 January 1955. NYC
Bud Powell Trio: Percy Heath (sbs); Kenny Clarke (dm)

2162-1	Mediocre	Verve MGV 8301
2163-1	All The Things You Are	—
2164-2	Epistrophy	Verve VE2 2526
2165-1	Dance Of The Infidels	Verve MGV 8301
2166-3	Salt Peanuts	—
2167-1	Hey George	—

25 April 1955. NYC
Bud Powell Trio: George Duvivier (sbs); Art Taylor (dm)

2322-1	Conception	Norgran MGN 1077
2333-1	Bean And The Boys	—
2333-4	Bean And The Boys	Verve VE2 2526
2334-4	Heart And Soul	Norgran MGN 1077
2335-2	Willow Groove	—
2336-1	Crazy Rhythm	—
2337-1	Willow Weep For Me	—
2338-1	East Of The Sun	Verve VE2 2526
2338-4	East Of The Sun (alt)	Norgran MGN 1077
2339-3	Lady Bird	Verve VE2 2526
2339-4	Lady Bird	Norgran MGN 1077
2340-1	Stairway To The Stars	—

27 April 1955. NYC
Bud Powell Trio: as 25 April

2341-4	Lullaby in Rhythm	Verve MGV 8301
2342-9	Star Eyes	—
2343-1	Confirmation	—

Early 1956. Birdland, NYC
Bud Powell Trio: Paul Chambers (sbs); Taylor (dm)
The session issued on Musidisc 30JA5167 and attributed to this personnel
and period is a reissue of the Pettiford–Haynes trio of 7 and 14 February
1953 and issued on Alto AL715.

13 September 1956. NYC
Bud Powell Trio: Ray Brown (sbs); Osie Johnson (dm)

4000-4	When I Fall In Love	Verve MGV 8218
4001-1	My Heart Stood Still	—
4002-1	Blues In The Closet	—
4003-4	Swingin' Til The Girls Come Home	—
4004-4	I Know That You Know	—
4005-1	Elegie	—
4006-2	Woody 'n' You	—
4007-2	I Should Care	—
4008-1	Now's The Time	—
4009-1	I Didn't Know What Time It Was	—
4010-1	Be Bop	—
4011-1	52nd St Theme	—

5 October 1956. NYC
Bud Powell Trio: Duvivier (sbs); Taylor (dm): *Strictly Powell*

G2JB7679-1	There Will Never Be Another You	Victor LPM 1423
G2JB7680-1	They Didn't Believe Me	—
G2JB7681-1	Lush Life	—
G2JB7682-2	Over The Rainbow	—
G2JB7683-1	I Cover The Waterfront	—
G2JB7684-1	Time Was	—
G2JB7685-1	Topsy Turvy	—
G2JB7686-1	Elegy	—
G2JB7687-3	Croscrane	—
G2JB7688-1	Jump City	—
G2JB7689-1	Blues For Bessie	—
G2JB7690	Lullaby To A Believer	(unissued)

11 February 1957. NYC
Bud Powell Trio: Duvivier (sbs); Taylor (dm): *Swingin' With Bud*

H2JB1578-8	Salt Peanuts	Victor LPM 1507
H2JB1579-1	Swedish Pastry	—
H2JB1580-1	Almost Like Being In Love	—
H2JB1581-1	Shaw 'Nuff	—
H2JB1582-4	Midway	—
H2JB1583-2	Oblivion	—
H2JB1584-1	Get It	—
H2JB1585-1	Another Dozen	—

H2JB1586-2	She	—
H2JB1587-3	In The Blue Of The Evening	—
H2JB1588-1	Birdland Blues	—

3 August 1957. Hackensack, NJ

Bud Powell Trio: Paul Chambers (sbs); Taylor (dm): *Bud! – The Amazing Bud Powell, iii*

Blue Pearl	Blue Note BLP 1571
Blue Pearl (alt)	Blue Note BST 84430
Keepin' In The Groove	Blue Note BLP 1571
Some Soul	—
Frantic Fancies	—
Bud On Bach (pno solo)	—

Same date. Same venue

Curtis Fuller (tmb) added

Idaho	Blue Note BLP 1571
Don't Blame Me	—
Moose The Mooche	—

25 May 1958. Hackensack, NJ

Bud Powell Trio: Sam Jones (sbs); Philly Joe Jones (dm): *Time Waits – The Amazing Bud Powell, iv*

John's Abbey (alt)	Blue Note BST 84430
Sub City (alt)	Blue Note BLP 1598
Sub City	—
John's Abbey	—
Buster Rides Again	—
Dry Soul	—
Marmalade	—
Monopoly	—
Time Waits	—

29 December 1958. Hackensack, NJ

Bud Powell Trio: Paul Chambers (sbs); Art Taylor (dm): *The Scene Changes – The Amazing Bud Powell, v*

The Scene Changes	Blue Note BLP 4009
Down With It	—
Comin' Up (alt)	Blue Note BST 84430
Comin' Up	Blue Note BLP 4009
Duid Deed	—
Cleopatra's Dream	—
Gettin' There	—
Crossin' The Channel	—
Danceland	—
Borderick	—

Late 1959. Paris

Bud Powell Quintet: Clark Terry (tpt); Barney Wilen (ts); Eric Peters

(sbs); Kenny Clarke (dm)
        No Problem   Europa Jazz EJ 1007
        Miguel's Party   —

12 December 1959. Paris
Bud Powell Quartet: Barney Wilen (ts); Pierre Michelot (sbs); Kenny Clarke (dm): *Bud In Paris*
        Shaw 'Nuff (trio)   Xanadu 102
        Oleo   —
        Autumn in New York   —
        John's Abbey   —

18 December 1959. Théâtre des Champs-Elysées, Paris
Paris Jam Session: Lee Morgan (tpt); Barney Wilen (as); Wayne Shorter (ts); Jymie Merritt (sbs); Art Blakey (dm)
        Dance Of The Infidels   Fontana 680207
        Bouncin' With Bud   —

14 February 1960. Paris
Bud Powell/Johnny Griffin: Griffin (ts)
        Idaho   Xanadu 102
        Perdido   —

12 March 1960. Paris
Bud Powell Trio: Michelot (sbs); Clarke (dm)
        Confirmation   Xanadu 102

2 April 1960. Grugahalle, Essen
Coleman Hawkins with the Oscar Pettiford Trio: Hawkins (ts); Pettiford (sbs); Clarke (dm)
        Yesterdays   Debut DEB131
        All The Things You Are —
        Stuffy   —
        Just You, Just Me   Fontana 688601ZL

Same date. Same venue
Oscar Pettiford Trio: as above, minus Hawkins
        Shaw 'Nuff   Fontana 688600ZL
        Willow Weep For Me   —
        John's Abbey   —
        Salt Peanuts   —
        Blues In The Closet   —
Some sources suggest Shaw 'Nuff *and* Blues In The Closet *were also recorded on this date by Powell, Michelot and Clarke, and these details appear on sleeves of Duke D 1012.*

15 June 1960. Paris
Bud Powell Trio: Michelot (sbs); Clarke (dm)
        Get Happy   Xanadu 102

13 July 1960. Antibes Jazz Festival, Juan-Les-Pins
Charles Mingus Sextet: Ted Curson (tpt); Eric Dolphy (as); Booker
Ervin (ts); Charles Mingus (sbs); Dannie Richmond (dm)
5265(37624)   I'll Remember April   Atlantic SD 2-3001

14 October 1960. Théâtre des Champs-Elysées, Paris
Bud Powell Trio: Michelot (sbs); Clarke (dm): *Memorial Oscar Pettiford*

Buttercup	Vogue EPL 7942
John's Abbey	—
Sweet And Lovely	—
Crossin' The Channel	—

14 March 1961. Essen
Bud Powell Trio: Michelot (sbs); Clarke (dm)
*This is a misattribution of the 2 April 1960 concert with Pettiford and
Clarke. Details associated with reissues such as Black Lion/Freedom
30125 are incorrect.*

? April 1961*. Blue Note Café, Paris
Bud Powell Trio: Michelot (sbs); Clarke (dm): *At The Blue Note Café*

There Will Never Be Another You	ESP Disk 1066
Thelonious	—
'Round Midnight	—
Night In Tunisia	—
Monk's Mood	—
Shaw 'Nuff	—
Lover Man	—
52nd St Theme	—

**There is some uncertainty about the date of this session. Most sources
prefer April 1961, but Schlouch dates it in 1962.*

? July 1961. Comblain-La-Tour, Belgium
Bud Powell Trio: Benoit Quersain (sbs); Joe Bourguignon (dm)
     I Remember Clifford   RCA LPM 10317

15 December 1961. Paris
Don Byas: Idrees Sulieman (tpt)*; Byas (ts); Michelot (sbs); Clarke
(dm): *A Tribute To Cannonball*

Just One Of Those Things	Columbia JC 35755
Jackie My Little Cat	—
Cherokee	—
I Remember Clifford	—
Good Bait*	—
Jeannine*	—
All The Things You Are*	—
Jackie	—

Myth*   —

17 December 1961. Paris
Bud Powell Trio: Michelot (sbs); Clarke (dm): *A Portrait Of Thelonious*
CO75895	Thelonious	Columbia CL2292
CO75896	Ruby My Dear	—
CO75897	There Will Never Be Another	
	You	—
CO75898	Off Minor	—
CO75899	I Ain't No Foolin'	—
CO75900	No Name Blues	—
CO75901	Squatty	—
CO75902	Monk's Mood	—
	Cherokee	(unissued)

19 April 1962. Golden Circle, Stockholm
Bud Powell Trio: Torbjörn Hultcrantz (sbs); Sune Spangberg (dm): *At The Golden Circle, Vol.1*
Move	Steeplechase 6001
Just A Gigolo	—
Relaxin' At The Camarillo	—
I Remember Clifford	—
Reets And I	—
Hackensack	—

At The Golden Circle, Vol.2
Like Someone In Love	Steeplechase 6002
I Hear Music	—
Moose The Mooche	—
Blues In The Closet	—
Star Eyes	—

23 April 1962. Golden Circle, Stockholm
Bud Powell Trio: Hultcrantz (sbs); Spangberg (dm): *At The Golden Circle, Vol 3*
Swedish Pastry	Steeplechase 6009
I Remember Clifford	—
I Hear Music	—

At The Golden Circle, Vol.4
Moose The Mooche	Steeplechase 6014
Star Eyes	—
Blues In The Closet	—
Reets And I	—
John's Abbey	—
Old Devil Moon	—

At The Golden Circle, Vol.5
Hot House	Steeplechase 6017

134

This Is No Laughing Matter	—
52nd St Theme	—
Straight No Chaser	—

26 April 1962. Copenhagen
Bud Powell Trio: Niels-Henning Ørsted Pedersen (sbs); William Schiøpffe (dm): *Bouncing With Bud*

I Remember Clifford	Sonet SLP 31
Rifftide	—
The Best Thing For You	—
Straight, No Chaser	—
Bouncin' With Bud	—
Hot House	—
Move	—
52nd St Theme	—
Ruby My Dear*	Delmark DL-406

Despite its listing in other published discographies, this track is not included on Sonet SLP 31.

3 January 1963. Koblenz
Bud Powell Trio: Jimmy Woode (sbs); Joe Harris (dm)

'Round Midnight	Impulse A(S) 36

Bud Powell Trio with Don Byas and Idrees Sulieman: as above, plus Sulieman (tpt)*; Byas (ts)

All The Things You Are*	Impulse A(S) 37
I Remember Clifford	—

Idrees Sulieman with Bud Powell Trio: as above, with Sulieman (tpt)

I Can't Get Started	Impulse A(S) 36

15 January 1963. Paris

Bud Powell Interview	Elektra Musician
	E1-60030

This date is clearly wrong. Paudras suggests in 'Danse des Infidèles' that it was conducted by Henri Renaud in mid-1963.

? February 1963. Paris
Bud Powell Trio: Gilbert Rovere (sbs); Kansas Fields (dm): *Bud Powell In Paris*

2439	How High The Moon	Reprise 6098
2440	Dear Old Stockholm	—
2441	Body And Soul	—
2442	Jordu	—
2443	Reets And I	—
2444	Satin Doll	—
2445	Parisian Thoroughfare	—
2446	I Can't Get Started	—
2447	Little Benny (Crazeology)	—

6 May 1963. Paris

Bud Powell interview	Elektra Musician E1-60030

The date of this interview is probably approximately one year later than this, which is the date given on the sleeve.

23 May 1963. CBS Studios, Paris

Dexter Gordon Quartet: Gordon (ts); Pierre Michelot (sbs); Kenny Clarke (dm): *Our Man In Paris*

Our Love Is Here To Stay	Blue Note BST 84430
Broadway	Blue Note BLP 4146
Stairway To The Stars	—
A Night In Tunisia	—
Willow Weep For Me	—
Scrapple From The Apple	—
Like Someone In Love (trio only)	Blue Note BST 84430

8 July 1963. Paris

Dizzy Gillespie et les Double Six: Gillespie (tpt); Michelot (sbs); Clarke (dm); Double Six Vocal Group*

29173	One Bass Hit	Philips PHM 200-106
29174	Two Bass Hit	—
29175	Emanon	—
29176	Blue 'n' Boogie	—
29177	The Champ	—
29178	Tin Tin Deo	—
29179	Groovin' High	—
29180	Ow!	—
29181	Hot House	—
29182	Anthropology	—

The vocal tracks were dubbed in a month later than the quartet recording.

31 July 1964. Paris

Bud Powell Trio: Michel Gaudry (sbs); Art Taylor (dm): *Blues For Bouffemont*

In The Mood For A Classic	Fontana SFJL901
Like Someone In Love	—
Una Noche Con Francis	—
Relaxin' At Camarillo	—
Blues For Bouffemont	—
Little Willie Leaps	—
My Old Flame	—
Moose The Mooche	—

? August 1964. Edenville, France

Bud Powell Trio and Johnny Griffin: Griffin (ts); Jacques Gervais (sbs); Guy Hayat (dm): *Hot House*

Straight No Chaser	Fontana FJL903

Salt Peanuts	—
Move	—
Bean And The Boys	—
Wee	—
Hot House	—
52nd St Theme (trio)	—
Body And Soul	Duke D1012
Blues	—

Various dates, 1962, 1963, 1964. Paris

Bud Powell At Home: Francis Paudras (brushes)*: *Strictly Confidential*

Cherokee*	Fontana 688318TL
My Devotion	—
Idaho*	—
Ruby My Dear	—
Conception*	—
All God's Children Got Rhythm*	—
Strictly Confidential*	—
Deep Night*	—
Thou Swell*	—
It Could Happen To You	—
Wahoo*	—

? September 1964. NYC

Bud Powell Trio: John Ore (sbs); J. C. Moses (dm): *Return*

I Know That You Know	Roulette 52115
Someone To Watch Over Me	—
The Best Thing For You	—
On Green Dolphin St	—
Just One Of Those Things	—
I Remember Clifford	—
Hallucinations	—
If I Loved You	—

Late 1964. New York

Bud Powell Trio: unknown (sbs, dm): *Ups 'n' Downs*

Ups And Downs	Mainstream MXRL385
Like Someone In Love	—
Earl's Improvisation	—
Thelonious	—
Moment's Notice	—
Caravan Riffs	—
'Round Midnight	—
Jazz Black And White	—
Buttercup	—
March To Paris	—

Schlouch dates this session as c.1960, Paris.

Late 1964. Englewood Cliffs, NJ
Bud Powell Trio: unknown (sbs); J. C. Moses (dm)
                Unknown titles   (unissued)

1 May 1965. Town Hall, NYC
Recording by ESP. Tape destroyed.

Late 1965. NYC
Bud Powell (solo pno)
                Unknown titles   ESP-Disk (unissued)

? January 1966. NYC
Bud Powell Trio: Scotty Holt (sbs); Rashied Ali (dm)
                Unknown titles   ESP-Disk (unissued)

BIBLIOGRAPHY

The following books and articles have been used in preparing the text. Some more general works are included, since they provide useful background detail.

Arnold William: *Shadowland* (New York, 1978)

Balliett, Whitney: *The Sound of Surprise* (New York, 1959)

Balliett, Whitney: *Ecstasy at the Onion* (New York and Indianapolis, 1971)

Barker, Danny: *A Life in Jazz*, edited by Alyn Shipton (London, 1986)

Barrett, Lindsay: 'About Bud Powell', *Jazz Journal* (June 1964) xvii/6

Burns, Jim: 'Early Stitt', *Jazz Journal* (October 1969) xxii/10

Butcher, Mike: 'Birdland '56 in Paris', *Jazz Journal* (date unknown, *c.* January 1957)

Chambers, Jack: *Milestones I: The Music and Times of Miles Davis to 1961* (Toronto, 1983)

Charters, Samuel B. and Kunstadt, Len: *Jazz: A History of the New York Scene* (Garden City, NY, 1962)

Collier, James L.:   *The Making of Jazz: A Comprehensive History* (New York, 1978)

Crawford, Marc: 'Requiem for a Heavyweight', *Down Beat* (20 October 1966)

Dance, Stanley: *The World of Duke Ellington* (New York, 1970)

Feather, Leonard: *The Encyclopedia of Jazz* (New York, 1955)

Feather, Leonard: *The Encyclopedia of Jazz in the Sixties* (New York, 1966)

Feather, Leonard and Gitler, Ira: *The Encyclopedia of Jazz in the Seventies* (New York, 1976)

Finch, Christopher: 'Growing Up With Bud', *Quest* (January/February 1978)

Fox, Charles: 'Max Roach', from *Repercussions: A Celebration of African-American Music*, edited by Geoffrey Haydon and Dennis Moody (London, 1985)

Gillespie, Dizzy with Fraser, Ali: *Dizzy: To Be Or Not To Bop. The Autobiography of Dizzy Gillespie* (Garden City, NY, 1979)

Ginibre, Jean-Louis: 'Kenny Clarke – de Pittsburgh à Montreuil', *Jazz Magazine* (March 1985) No.337

Gitler, Ira: *Jazz Masters of the Forties* (New York, 1966)

Gitler, Ira: *Swing To Bop: An Oral History of the Transition of Jazz in the 1940s* (New York and Oxford, 1985)

Goddard, Chris: *Jazz Away From Home* (London, 1979)

Harrison, Max; Morgan, Alun; Atkins, Ronald; James, Michael; and Cooke, Jack: *Modern Jazz: 1945-1970: The Essential Records: A Critical Selection* (London, 1975)

Hentoff, Nat: *The Jazz Life* (London, 1961)

Hentoff, Nat: *Jazz Is* (London, 1976)

Horricks, Raymond: *These Jazzmen of our Time* (London, 1960)

Horricks, Raymond: 'Bud Powell – Tragedy of a Giant', *Jazz Monthly* (July 1955) i/5

James, Michael: *Ten Modern Jazzmen* (London, 1960)

Kernfeld, Barry, ed.: *The New Grove Dictionary of Jazz* (London 1988)

Korall, Burt: 'View from the Seine', *Down Beat* (5 December 1963)

Levitt, Al: 'Les Silences de Bud', *Jazz Magazine* (May 1980) No.286

McCarthy, Albert: *Big Band Jazz* (New York and London, 1974)

Mohr, Kurt: 'Le Grand Bud', *Le Jazz Hot* (date unknown, *c.*1960)

Morrison, Alan: 'Can a Musician Return from the Brink of Insanity?', *Ebony* (August 1953)

Paudras, Francis: *La Danse des Infidèles* (Paris, 1986)

Perlongo, Robert A.: 'Bud Powell in Paris', *Metronome* (November 1961)

Priestley, Brian: *Charles Mingus: A Critical Biography* (London, 1982)

Priestley, Brian: *Charlie Parker* (Tunbridge Wells, 1984)

Réda, Jacques: 'La Force de Bud Powell', *Jazz Magazine* (May 1980) No.286

Reisner, Robert: *Bird: The Legend of Charlie Parker* (New York, 1962)

Rosenwaike, Ira: *Population History of New York City* (New York, 1972)

Russell, Ross: *Bird Lives! The High Life and Hard Times of Charlie 'Yardbird' Parker* (New York, 1973)

Shapiro, Nat and Hentoff, Nat: *Hear Me Talkin' To Ya!* (New York, 1955)

Simon, George T.:   *The Big Bands* (New York, 1967)

Spellman, A. B.:   *Four Lives in the Bebop Business* (New York, 1966)

Taylor, Arthur: *Notes and Tones: Musician to Musician Interviews* (Liège, Belgium, 1977)

Wagner, Jean: 'Enquête: Boulevard de Crépuscule', *Jazz Magazine* (date unknown, c.1963)

Zannini, Marcel: 'Le Dernier Chorus du Bird', *Le Jazz Hot* (c.May 1955)

The illustrations used in this book come from the Max Jones Collection, the Frank Driggs collection, Andre Sas, and from stills used to promote records made or distributed by Blue Note Records, Impulse and Prestige. Pictures are reproduced by courtesy of Richard Anderson, Herve Derrien, Europress, Flair Photography, Hans Harzheim, *Jazz Journal International*, Jazz Music Books, Howard Lucraft, *Melody Maker, Rhythm*, Andrew E. Salmieri, Heine Wederhake and Valerie Wilmer.

Although efforts have been made to trace the present copyright holders of photographs, the publishers apologize for any unintentional omission or neglect and will be pleased to insert the appropriate acknowledgements to companies or individuals in any subsequent edition of this book.

INDEX